THE MEAT TEACHER COOKBOOK

THE MEAT TEACHER COOKBOOK

The Ultimate Backyard
BBQ Guide for
an A+ in Pitmastery!

MATT GROARK

WITH PHOTOGRAPHY BY KRISTIN GROARK

HARPER INFLUENCE
An Imprint of HarperCollins*Publishers*

To my vegetable-loving wife, Kristin, and my meat-loving boys, Aidric and Nash, you are my motivation and inspiration. I love you so much!

To Poppa G, you showed me what family, service, community, and a damn good tailgate are all about. Without you, none of this happens. "30 Up!" GO BIRDS!

CONTENTS

My Story   1

Period 1   Homeroom: Grilling 101   15

Period 2   The Big Three: Pork, Beef, and Chicken   25

Period 3   Meat of the Sea: Seafood   103

Period 4   Wild Game: Lamb, Veal, and Elk   123

Period 5   Get Sauced: Sauces, Rubs, and Spices   143

Period 6   On the Sideline: BBQ Side Dishes   155

Period 7   Sweet Tooth: Desserts   179

Period 8   Extracurricular Activities: Tailgating and Camping   199

Extra Credit   Vegetarian Grilling   223

Acknowledgments   245

Index   246

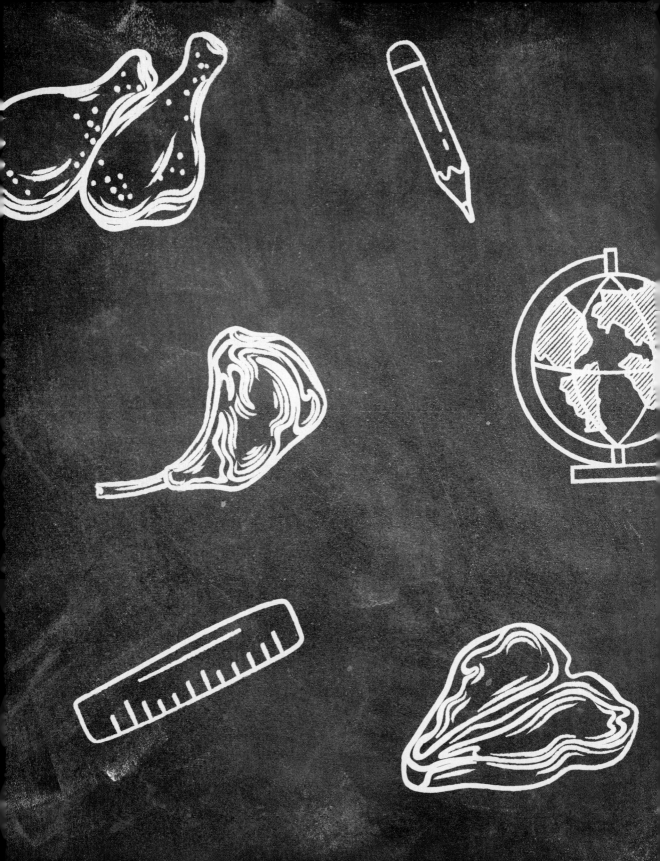

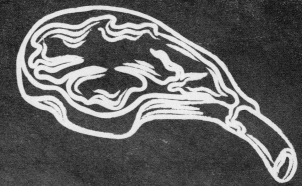

THE MEAT TEACHER COOKBOOK

Many chefs tell the heartwarming story of how their passion and excitement for food began in their mother's kitchen. They have tear-jerking memories of learning family secrets, tasting new flavors, and eventually being entrusted with handwritten recipes scribbled on scrap paper and passed down from generation to generation.

That's not how my story goes.

My memories of food as a kid involved either takeout or delivery. On a nightly basis, my dad, brother, and I would choose either pizza, Chinese food, or a bucket of fried chicken. Don't get me wrong, it was every kid's dream, and I wouldn't have changed a thing. But my story of falling in love with food began much later in life and not in my mother's kitchen, but in an empty Philadelphia parking lot at 6 a.m. on a Sunday.

My obsession for outdoor grilling started with tailgating at Eagles games. I took command of planning the menu, shopping, prepping, and packing the coolers with food so it was ready to hit the grill. I proudly served breakfast, followed by some finger foods and appetizers, culminating in charcoal-grilled tomahawk steaks or slow-cooked baby back ribs. I was the master of the grill and would make it my mission to feed everyone in the parking lot. However, it wasn't until I was gifted my first smoker from my father-in-law that my love of BBQ truly ignited!

The very next morning after receiving the smoker, I was up before the sun and had my new smoker filled with every type of meat I could find. In those first few months, I smoked everything you could imagine. I had some victories and many defeats. Sometimes the result was a perfectly executed, tender, and juicy pulled pork. Others, it was a tough, rubbery brisket. There were a few tears, but every time, I learned. After months of watching from a distance, my wife, Kristin, decided it was time for me to learn from a master. Ironically, my sweet vegetarian wife surprised me with a weekend trip to a BBQ class by Myron Mixon, the winningest man in BBQ. I can look back on that weekend as the moment that BBQ went from being my hobby to my lifestyle.

At this point in my life, I was a high school physical education teacher of fifteen years. While Kristin and I were busy raising our two young boys, Aidric and Nash, I always had several side hustles going to help make ends meet. I waited tables, coached basketball, and risked life and limb teaching inexperienced teenagers how to drive. I

constantly heard "It must be so nice to have summers off," knowing full well I never did.

But the more I cooked in my backyard, the better my BBQ got. And the more people I fed, the more they kept coming back. Before I knew it, people were paying me for what I was cooking. Finally, I had a side hustle that I was not only passionate about, but that also paid some bills.

In a matter of a few years, I went from being a teacher practicing and hustling BBQ out of my backyard, to owning a thirty-foot BBQ rig and cooking at festivals for thousands of people, to shaking hands with Gordon Ramsay on the set of *Next Level Chef*. It's pretty unbelievable—and still feels pretty surreal. If you're wondering how this kind of leap is even possible, well, the answer lies in just two words: SOCIAL MEDIA! When I started my grilling journey, TikTok didn't exist, YouTube was only long-form video, Facebook was for "old people," and Instagram was a platform for photography. Thankfully, I was starting to make good-looking and delicious food, so I started taking pictures and sharing them with my modest following. Not long after those initial posts, I discovered that BBQ had a very loyal and committed community, and I began amassing more and more dedicated followers each day. However, I didn't realize exactly HOW loyal and life-changing social media communities could be until my high school students helped my wife and me through a very difficult time. We had just suffered our last of five miscarriages. I missed some time from school. When I returned, I sat down with all of my students and very openly explained the situation my wife and I were dealing with. It was actually a very teachable moment, considering I was teaching Health Education at the time. A couple days later, before class, I was greeted with a card, two 76ers tickets, and a note:

"We know you are in a very tough place right now and we want to show our thanks for you using this situation as an example and teaching us to keep your head up even when life hits rock bottom. Here's two tickets for you and your wife, hope this takes your mind off things for a bit."

It was easily the kindest gesture I'd ever experienced, and it was from a group of teenagers.

I'm sure you can relate to the metaphor about momentum and how things can "snowball," but for the sake of our BBQ theme, let's say that things "caught fire" at this point. As their teacher, I was incredibly proud of their kindness, and I wanted to share

NASH

AIDRIC

FOOD FUN FAMILY

GROARK BOYS
BBQ

WE DO THE WORK! YOU HAVE THE FUN!
WWW.GROARKBOYSBBQ.COM

what they had done with the community. I posted the brief story alongside a photo of the card, and it went viral! Before I knew it, the Philadelphia 76ers reached out, and with their help, we turned the game into a field trip and my entire class came with us. The story was subsequently picked up by all local news stations, flooded social media platforms, and went national. Soon, my inbox blew up with messages from people across the country sending love and praising my students.

One very special email came from a meat wholesaler in California, Premier Meat Company. They reached out and offered to fund a BBQ for my whole school—so a BBQ is exactly what we did! I had one stipulation. I asked if we could turn it into a fundraiser and donate the proceeds to charity. Thanks to my students and the support of my new BBQ community, we organized my first fundraising event and donated over $3,000 to charity. After starting Groark Boys BBQ as a means to run this fundraiser, many more followed, and in my first year of business, we ended up donating over $30,000 to charities such as Operation Smile (our son Aidric was born with a cleft lip and palate), the MS Foundation, and Epilepsy Research, along with several veteran organizations. All of this stemmed from a single act of kindness from my students.

After this explosion of popularity and media attention, figuring out how to juggle my teaching career and a newfound BBQ business became a challenge. I was busy catering for parties, bringing my food truck to events, and continuing to feed first responders in my community. Then a new social media platform made its debut and changed my life forever. In December 2018, I posted my first video on TikTok. Months went by without much traction, until I posted a video about making "The Perfect Steak," and it went viral! I was blown away by the response, but as far as the comments were concerned, not all were nice. This was my first true lesson in social media. Comments are not always supportive and at times can be downright brutal. If you do "go viral," it's usually because your comments are being flooded with negativity and a whole lot of people who obviously know more than you do. But I didn't let it stop me, and I continued to make videos and post content.

My following was increasing by the thousands and then the millions. And the more people started tuning in to my content, the more inspired I was to not only help teach people how to cook delicious food, but to feed them delicious food as well. Before I knew it, I had an agent and multiple brand deals and signed contracts with major food-

based corporations across the country and beyond. My BBQ side hustle had become a full-time career in food!

It was more than I could have ever asked for—but little did I know that the true pivotal moment in my career was yet to come. In the fall of 2023, I received life-changing news: I was selected to compete with seventeen other chefs on Gordon Ramsay's *Next Level Chef* on FOX! Here I was, a teacher and dad from New Jersey, who fell in love with BBQ in his backyard, now competing on a cooking television show created by the biggest food celebrity in the world. To top it off, the show premiered right after the Super Bowl. And you can guess who was playing—the Philadelphia Eagles, of course! Unfortunately, we didn't win, but wow, to think about my beginnings in a Philly tailgate parking lot at 6 a.m. to following the Eagles in the Super Bowl on prime-time TV.

Fast-forward to today and that "side hustle" is now a successful BBQ brand where I get to cook, feed, and create content for over five million of you across platforms! Not only that, but my school district asked me to make the jump from PE teacher to culinary arts instructor, which, you can imagine, combines the best of both worlds for me. Figuring out how to teach full-time, sell BBQ, create content, and spend quality time with my family sometimes seems like an impossible task. But I'm continuing to figure it out. It's also why you'll see that many of the recipes in this book are quick, easy, and VERY approachable, so you can enjoy BBQ with your family, friends, and community without losing hours of time by the smoker.

These recipes are the beginning of a tradition that I never had growing up. So much of my time in the kitchen or backyard is with my family and friends and now my students! Whether it's creating a vegetarian-friendly meal with Kristin, grilling the perfect steak with Aidric and Nash, or learning a new recipe and experimenting alongside my students, my time spent around food is always filled with so much joy. I hope you can find that same joy from these pages as creating them has brought me! While my journey is not a traditional one, it stands as a testament to the power of hard work, passion, and a healthy dose of motivation provided by one of the most amazing communities there is. The most exciting part? I may be a teacher, but I would not be here without also being a great student. You see, the learning never ends when it comes to food, so I'm encouraged that our story together is just beginning!

MY FOOD PHILOSOPHY: FOOD, FUN, FAMILY!

Through my twenty-year career as a high school teacher, the best interests of my students are at the forefront of every decision I make. The weekly and sometimes daily transition from high school teacher to Meat Teacher can at times be exhausting and challenging. However, when wearing both hats, I embrace the role of educator. Every recipe I cook, every event I serve, and every video I post is done with my reader, customer, and viewer in mind.

My hope is that this book lays a very solid foundation for that lesson and encourages you to get in your backyard and behind your grill to begin bringing out the best that food has to offer you and your community.

GRILLING 101

"FAIL TO PREPARE, PREPARE TO FAIL"

I have carried this quote with me throughout my teaching career, and I do the same when cooking. If you walk into a classroom of thirty-plus high school kids without a plan, you will fail. The same goes in the kitchen or behind the grill. Now, being unprepared is very different from making a mistake. Mistakes happen, and at the end of the day, we learn from them. I learn EVERY DAY!

As a teacher, first period is always the most important part of my day because it sets the tone. The list below will set the tone for your backyard BBQ journey. And remember: There will be mistakes along the way, but you will be prepared!

MUST-KNOW VOCABULARY

- **Pitmaster:** The sweaty, greasy, meat- and smoke-smelling badass who presides over the fire to create the perfectly charred and tender protein of your dreams!
- **Indirect or Direct, Two-Zone Cooking:** Possibly the most important cooking technique you can learn on the grill. This method involves dividing your cooking surface into a direct cooking area (HOT ZONE) and an indirect cooking area (LESS HOT ZONE) in order to maintain more control of the temperature and cook the interior and exterior of the meat separately.
- **Bark:** The dark, outer layer that is formed by the combination of spice rub and slow smoking. This layer is extremely flavorful and sometimes is also referred to as the "crust."

- **Carryover:** When meat is cooked and removed from the heat, the cooking process continues because the exterior of the food is hot and the heat continues to carry over and cook the interior. As a rule, a thick piece of meat will continue to carry over for approximately 15 minutes and increase internal temperature by 5 to 10 degrees.
- **Rub:** The combination of spices used to season your meat!
- **Binder:** This can be a contentious topic, as some are of the opinion that binders are unnecessary. A binder is used on meat to help the rub adhere. The most common binder I use for barbecuing is mustard. It doesn't add flavor but does wonders in helping the rub adhere and to create a beautiful bark. Other binders include oil, mayo, and hot sauce, to name a few.

BACKYARD SUPPLY LIST

- **Smoker:** A smoker is used to cook meat, fish, and other foods slowly, at a low temperature, typically for several hours. Smokers are designed to impart a smoky flavor to the food by burning wood chips or chunks.
- **Grill:** Typically used outdoors, a grill uses direct heat to cook food. Grills are most commonly used for barbecuing and grilling. They can use various fuel sources, such as gas, charcoal, or wood pellets.
- **Lighter:** In order to start a fire in a grill or smoker, you'll need a lighter to ignite a flame. If you want to level up a little, look into a torch such as the Grill Gun or Rocket Fire Torch.
- **Meat Thermometer:** This tool is used to measure the internal temperature of meat and other cooked foods. It helps ensure that the food is cooked to the desired level of doneness and is safe to eat.
- **Charcoal:** Charcoal is a black, porous substance made by burning wood in the absence of oxygen. Thanks to its high heat output and long-lasting burn, it's commonly used as a fuel source for grills and smokers.
- **Wood:** In the context of outdoor cooking, wood refers to specific types of hardwoods or fruitwoods that are used to generate smoke and flavor when cooking

on a grill or smoker. Different types of wood will impart different flavors to the food.

- **Heat-Resistant Gloves:** Unsurprisingly, things get pretty hot when you're grilling and smoking. Heat-resistant gloves are protective gloves designed to withstand high temperatures and are crucial when you're handling hot grates, pans, or other objects in outdoor cooking to prevent burns and injuries.

- **Tools (spatula, tongs, etc.):** There are various utensils and tools used for cooking on a grill or smoker. Spatulas are used for flipping food, tongs are used for gripping and turning food, and other tools such as brushes and skewers may be used for specific cooking tasks.

- **Trash Bags:** Outdoor cooking can get messy, so make sure you have trash bags on hand to collect and dispose of waste such as food scraps and packaging.

- **Aluminum Foil:** Thin, flexible, and easy to use, aluminum foil is commonly used in outdoor cooking to wrap food for grilling or smoking to create a sealed environment, which helps retain moisture and flavor.

- **Grill Brush:** A grill brush is a cleaning tool used to remove food residue, grease, and debris from the grates of a grill. The only one I use and recommend is the BBQ DADDY by Scrub Daddy.

SAFETY FIRST

- **First-Aid Kit:** A good old-fashioned home kit will be perfect. Make sure you have burn gel and gauze. Grilling can be a dangerous and risky game, so you want to prepare for everything.

- **Extinguisher:** When playing with fire—even in your own backyard—it's a good idea to have one on hand. A class K extinguisher will offer the most control for cooking fires involving grease.

- **Grill Cleaner/Degreaser:** A clean grill is a safe grill. The more you cook on your grill, the dirtier it will get. Built-up grease and grime are a dangerous thing, as it increases your chances of having flare-ups. I recommend cleaning the grates after every cook and making sure grease traps and deflectors are cleaned at least every

other cook. A grill covered in food and grease is not "a well-seasoned grill," it's a dirty and dangerous one!

- **Sunscreen:** BBQ and grilling are obviously done outdoors, so be sure to take care of your skin. I credit this recommendation to my wife!

- **Bug Spray:** Not typically something you would think to have handy while working the grill, but I promise you will thank me later.

BASIC MEAT TEMPERATURE CHART

MEAT	TEMPERATURES
Steak/Beef/Elk/Lamb/Veal	
Rare	120°F–125 °F (48.9°C to 51.6°C)
Medium-rare	130°F–135°F (54.4°C–57.2°C)
Medium	140°F–145°F (60°C–62.8°C)
Medium-well	150°F–155°F (65.5°C–68.3°C)
Well done	160°F (71.1°C) and above
Chicken	165°F–175°F (73.9°C–80°C)
Pork	145°F (62.8°C)
Fish and Shellfish	145°F (62.8°C)
Reheated Leftovers	165°F (73.9°C)
Holding Temperature for Cooked Food	140°F (60°C)

BBQ TIPS EVERYONE SHOULD KNOW

- **Smoker:** Every smoker is different, so make sure you're familiar with yours. Identify the hot spots. You can do this by performing the "biscuit test." All you

need is a roll of biscuits and your grill. Spread the biscuits around the cooking surface, leaving some space between them. Make sure the entire surface of your smoker is covered, including the center, sides, and any additional racks. Set your smoker to 250°F and set a timer for 30 minutes. When time is up, open your grill and observe the differences in the biscuits. Biscuits in hotter areas will be darker and more cooked, while lower sections may be lighter and undercooked. A few degrees can make a difference during cooking, so note these spots and adjust your process accordingly.

- **Direct vs. Indirect:** Here's my simple rule of thumb when deciding on a direct or indirect cook: If the food takes less than 20 minutes to cook, use direct heat. If it is a longer cook, use indirect heat. Let's use chicken as an example. If I'm cooking chicken thighs, I'm using direct grilling, while a whole chicken will be cooked with the indirect method.

- **Homemade Grill Brush:** No grill brush and a dirty grill? No fear. Grab a few sheets of aluminum foil and crumple them into a ball. Use a pair of tongs to hold the foil and scrape it across the grill to remove any unwanted nasty bits!

- **Let It Rest:** In all honestly, if I grill a steak and I'm starving, I eat it immediately. But when I can help it, letting meat rest is the way to go. As a general rule, the bigger the steak, the longer the rest. A 1-inch ribeye should be rested between 5 and 10 minutes. A 3-inch-thick cut bone-in ribeye should be rested for 10 to 12 minutes. A whole chicken should be rested for 15 minutes. Prime rib gets 45 minutes to 1 hour. The resting time gives the juices time to redistribute throughout the meat.

- **Know Your Temperatures:** This goes for your grill and your food. For searing and achieving that coveted char, you'll want a high heat (around 450 to 500°F). For more delicate items like fish and veggies, aim for medium heat (around 350°F). And for low and slow cooking (think BBQ), stick to a lower heat (around 225 to 275°F). As far as your meat temperatures, different proteins have different recommended temperatures: see the chart on page 20.

- **Smoke 'em if ya got 'em:** Add smoke to a cook regardless of what you are cooking on. If using charcoal, add wood chunks on top. If cooking on a gas grill, you can use a tube smoker or a pouch of foil with wood chips and holes poked in the top. Regardless of what you are cooking on, you can always add that smoky flavor!

@groarkboysbbq
Pig Shots Demo

Period 2
THE BIG THREE

PORK, BEEF, AND CHICKEN

The morning after my father-in-law gifted me my first smoker—also known as the day that my real BBQ journey began—I headed straight to the grocery store and loaded my cart with an array of meats. I didn't know where to begin, and my knowledge of smoking meats was rudimentary at best, but I knew enough to focus on what I now affectionally call the "Big Three": pork, beef, and chicken.

The Big Three represent the heart and soul of BBQ—from pulled pork, to brisket, to smoked chicken, these meats are the mouthwatering building blocks of any grilling adventure. Mastering the Big Three was no easy feat, but each rubbery brisket and too-dry chicken taught me valuable lessons. Soon enough, I learned how to control all the different BBQ variables, like temperature control, wood selection, timing, and marinades.

As the Meat Teacher, I knew I had to kick off this cookbook with a crash course on the staples. In Period 2, you'll find the tips and tricks I've learned (along with my favorite recipes, of course) so you can master the Big Three, too!

PORK

Some cuts of pork, like a pork tenderloin or a beautiful pork chop, can be challenging and take precise timing and temperature to get right. Others, like pork belly and pork butt, allow for some wiggle room as you learn the process of time and temperature. For that reason, pork is always the protein I suggest people learn first when they're starting out in the world of BBQ. It's delicious, forgiving, and extremely versatile, so fire up your smoker or grill and dive right in!

- Groark Boys Pulled Pork
- Grilled Pork Chops with Pineapple-Ginger Glaze
- Stuffed Pork Loin with Maple Dijon Glaze
- Smoked Pickle-Glazed Baby Back Ribs
- Pork Belly Burnt Ends
- Dry-Rubbed Pork Tenderloin
- Grilled Pork Steaks
- Al Pastor–Style Pulled Pork
- "Brisket"-Style Pork Belly

GROARK BOYS PULLED PORK

SERVES 15 TO 18

"I just got a smoker, and I am new to it. What should I cook first?"

This is by far the most common question I get. My answer is quite simple, and it is always the same: PORK BUTT! The reason is not only simple but sensible. Pork butt is one of the most forgiving pieces of meat in BBQ. Its amount of fat makes it very hard to dry out. There is room for some error without ruining the end product. The same cannot be said for many of the other proteins in this book.

Pulled pork was the first meat I cooked on my very first smoker and easily the most popular menu item on the Groark Boys BBQ rig. While this recipe is ideal for a smoker, it can also be adapted to a gas grill or oven. You can use it to make a classic pulled pork sandwich topped with my spicy, crunchy Smack Slaw (page 156) or even as a topping for nachos and pizza. It is also perfect for a large party or for creative and easy family meals. Consider this pulled pork recipe your intro to BBQ!

One 6- to 8-pound bone-in Boston butt

2 tablespoons yellow mustard

6 tablespoons Sweet and Spicy Pork Rub (page 150)

1 cup apple juice

1. Preheat your grill or smoker to 300°F for indirect heat (cold side and hot side). We are going hot and fast! While traditional BBQ is "low and slow," I like to cook this recipe at a higher temperature and for a shorter amount of time because the high fat content makes this the perfect vessel for the hot and fast method.

2. This is optional: Score the pork butt's fat cap by slicing shallow, thin parallel lines 1 inch apart from each other along the fat. Turn the pork butt 45 degrees and create the same slices, producing a checkerboard effect.

3. Using a brush or your fingers, spread the mustard over the entire pork shoulder and rub with the rub.

4. Place the pork on the cold side of the grill or smoker and cook for 3 to 4 hours, until the internal temperature reaches 165°F. To best measure internal temperature, place a wireless or digital temperature probe into the thickest part of the pork butt.

5. Line a large, deep aluminum pan with a 12 x 12-inch sheet of aluminum foil or use a disposable aluminum half pan. Place the pork in the pan and pour the apple juice into the base of the pan. Tear another large sheet of aluminum foil and seal the pan by wrapping the pan with the foil, or wrap the foil around the pan and crimp the edges tightly.

6. Place the pan back on the grill or smoker until the internal temperature of the pork butt reaches 203°F, roughly another 2 hours.

7. TIME TO REST! Not you, the pork! Minimum 3 hours. If you own an insulated hot box (I prefer the Cambro GoBox!), use it, but a cooler will also work. If you are using a cooler, preheat it by placing a pot of boiling water inside and leaving it for 10 minutes. Place the foiled pork in a heavy towel and place it in the preheated cooler.

8. Now for the FUN! This is the payoff for all your time and energy! You will be pulling the blade bone. Pulling this bone out easily and clean with no meat stuck to it is the best marker of a perfectly cooked pork butt. It will still be too hot to touch, so a pair of nitrile gloves over cotton gloves works perfectly. A couple forks can get the job done, too. Don't forget to save the rendered juices to mix with the pork—I call it liquid gold!

9. If you have a large amount of pulled pork, divide it into smaller portions. This will make it easier to reheat only what you need later, reducing the risk of food waste. Place in airtight containers or resealable plastic bags. Make sure there's minimal air inside the container, as air can promote freezer burn or spoilage. Always label the containers or bags with the date you cooked the pork. This helps you keep track of its freshness.

Cheat Sheet

- Refrigeration: If you plan to eat the pork within 3 to 4 days, store it in the refrigerator at a temperature of 40°F or below. Place it on the shelves, not in the door, as the door is subject to temperature fluctuations.

    – Freezing: If you won't be using the leftovers within 3 to 4 days, consider freezing it. Use a freezer-safe container or bag and remove as much air as possible. Store it in the freezer at 0°F or lower, where it will keep for 2 to 6 months.

    – By preheating your cooler, you are creating an environment that will maintain a safe holding temperature, as opposed to placing the pork into a cold or room-temperature environment.

    – Shredding is a matter of choice. I prefer some nice-sized chunks in my pulled pork, whereas some like theirs very finely shredded. Completely and totally up to you!

- If you choose not to score your meat, no matter—I've found it doesn't make much of a difference. Opinions on this vary greatly, though. Some will say scoring adds flavor because you're able to get the seasoning deeper into the meat. Some will say it is mostly aesthetic. Both can be true—it is up to you. The reason I don't score is because I am a firm believer in seasoning your meat *after* you pull it. With such a large piece of meat, introducing that "liquid gold" and reseasoning makes all the difference. BLAND FOOD IS BAD!

GRILLED PORK CHOPS WITH PINEAPPLE-GINGER GLAZE

SERVES 4

If your top priority is preventing a dry and overcooked pork chop, this recipe is the place to start. While your instinct may be to go with boneless chops because they are cheaper, know that it's the bone that is going to keep these chops moist and tender. Combined with a glaze of pineapple juice and ginger, the only regret here will be that you did not double the recipe! Thicker is better for this recipe, so I recommend using 1 to 1½-inch chops. The "just keep flipping" method is the key to ensuring an even sear while being able to closely monitor the internal temperature of your meat. This method also works great for cooking beef and lamb.

¾ cup packed brown sugar

½ cup pineapple juice

½ teaspoon ground ginger

Four 1- to 1½-inch bone-in pork loin chops

1 teaspoon kosher salt

1 teaspoon freshly ground black pepper

1 tablespoon avocado oil or another neutral oil

1. Preheat your grill to medium heat.

2. Begin by making the glaze. Whisk the brown sugar, pineapple juice, and ground ginger in a small bowl and set aside.

3. To prep the pork, make 3 little slices that run vertical to the bone in the fat cap. This will prevent the chop from bending while it grills, which would result in an uneven sear.

4. Combine the salt and pepper in a small bowl. Brush your pork chops with the oil and season with the salt and pepper mixture.

5. Place the pork chops on the grill. We are using the "just keep flipping" method and will flip every 30 seconds until we reach the desired doneness of an internal temperature of 140°F. Begin by flipping four times: 30 seconds, flip, 30 seconds, flip, 30 seconds, flip, 30 seconds, flip. After the fourth flip, begin brushing the pork with the glaze and continue to flip and glaze every 30 seconds until you reach an internal temperature of 140°F in the thickest part of the chop. Be patient with the glaze—introducing it too early could result in the sugars burning.

6. Remove the pork chops and let rest for 10 minutes. This will allow the juices to redistribute and the internal temperature to reach 145°F. You want the juices in the pork, not on the cutting board! You will finish with perfectly caramelized, moist, and tender pork chops.

CHEAT SHEET

REST: We will come back to this time and time again! Refusing to properly rest your meat can mean all that hard work and effort is for naught. Resting is essential for carryover cooking and ensures your end product is juicy and flavorful.

STUFFED PORK LOIN
WITH **MAPLE DIJON GLAZE**

SERVES 8

During the holiday season, people constantly ask me if I plan on smoking my turkey. The answer is *of course*, but recently I've taken a step back from the traditional turkey, glazed ham, and prime rib. In search of a more creative approach to the holidays, I could think of none other than one of the most slept-on proteins and best part of the hog: the pork loin! Butterflied, stuffed, and with all the flavors of the holidays, this recipe is a showstopper to place front and center for even the fanciest holiday spreads.

For the Stuffing:

1 teaspoon canola oil

½ pound bratwurst sausage

¼ cup chopped walnuts

¼ cup craisins

1 Granny Smith apple, cored and diced

1 tablespoon butter

1 cup panko breadcrumbs

¼ cup apple juice, plus more as needed

Kosher salt and freshly ground black pepper

For the Pork:

One 3-pound center-cut pork loin

Butcher's twine (about five 12-inch strings)

1. Preheat your smoker to 250°F using your wood of choice. I prefer lighter woods, like apple and hickory, to avoid overpowering the palate.

2. Make the stuffing: Heat the oil in a large sauté pan over medium-high heat.

3. Remove the casings from the bratwurst and discard them, then add the bratwurst to the pan. Cook, stirring to break up the meat, for 3 to 5 minutes, until browned, then remove the bratwurst from the pan to a bowl and set aside (make sure to save the fat in the pan!).

4. To the same pan, add the walnuts, craisins, and apples and cook for 2 to 3 minutes, until the apples start to soften. Add the butter and cook until the apples are softened, 3 to 5 minutes.

5. Return the bratwurst to the pan, add the panko, and stir to combine for 30 seconds.

6. Add the apple juice, adding more as needed and being mindful of consistency (think Thanksgiving stuffing). Season with salt and pepper.

7. Remove from the heat, cool, then cover and refrigerate for 1 hour. Using cold stuffing makes the stuffing process simpler and is nice for advance prep—you can make it up to 4 days ahead.

For the Glaze:

½ cup real maple syrup

2 tablespoons Dijon mustard

1 tablespoon soy sauce

1 tablespoon apple cider vinegar

Kosher salt and freshly ground
 black pepper

8. While the stuffing cools, butterfly the pork loin so you end up with one flat piece—I like to use a mallet or small pot to pound the pork flat so it's uniform and cooks more evenly. Trim any unwanted silver skin and fat, then square up the corners and sides and season evenly with salt and pepper.

9. Remove the stuffing from the refrigerator and spread it onto the pork loin, leaving about 1 inch from the sides and corners.

10. Time to ROLL! Starting on the side without the fat cap, roll up, using butcher's twine, starting at one end and trussing about 2 inches apart across the length of the loin. You want the fat cap exposed on the outside of the roll. Finish with salt and pepper on the outside of the loin.

11. Put the pork on the smoker and cook to an internal temperature of 140°F, 1 to 1½ hours. I recommend using a digital meat thermometer such as the MEATER Plus.

12. Remove the pork from the smoker and tent loosely with foil for 15 to 20 minutes. This will allow juices to redistribute.

13. While the pork is resting, prepare the glaze by whisking the maple syrup, mustard, soy sauce, and vinegar in a small pot over medium-high heat. Season with salt and pepper, remove from the heat, and let cool.

14. Brush glaze over the pork. Place the pork loin back on the smoker for 5 to 10 minutes for the glaze to set and get nice and tacky. Slice and serve.

CHEAT SHEET

For extra flavor and color, sear the stuffed pork loin in a hot skillet or on a grill for a few minutes on all sides before smoking. This helps to caramelize the exterior and lock in the juices.

SMOKED PICKLE-GLAZED BABY BACK RIBS

SERVES 2

Growing up in south Jersey, there was nothing like a backyard BBQ on my street. Parents blasting golden oldies, kids in the pool, and the smell of some baby back ribs on the grill. This recipe brings back these memories like it was yesterday. For a fresh twist to this nostalgic classic, we are ditching the BBQ sauce and bringing the fresh and slightly tangy taste of dill pickle to the party!

1 rack baby back pork ribs

2 tablespoons yellow mustard

½ cup Sweet and Spicy Pork Rub (page 150)

½ cup strained dill pickle juice

1 cup light brown sugar

1. Preheat your smoker to 300°F. I like to use applewood when smoking pork for a subtle smoked flavor.

2. Remove the membrane from the ribs by sliding a butter knife underneath the thin white membrane that is on the bone side of the ribs. A dry towel will help you grip while you pull it away from the meat. Don't skip this step—if it's not removed, the membrane can be a rather unpleasant mouthfeel.

3. Pat your ribs dry with a paper towel. Apply a thin layer of mustard to the ribs and season both sides of the rack with the rub.

4. When the smoker reaches 300°F and the smoke is running clear, place the ribs on the smoker bone-side down. Grab a drink and prepare the glaze!

5. In a small pot, combine the strained pickle juice and brown sugar, place over medium-high heat, and whisk for 1 minute, making sure the sugar is fully dissolved. Drop

the heat to low and simmer for 5 minutes. Remove from the heat and let cool. The glaze should be shiny and still fairly loose—it will thicken slightly as it cools.

6. At the 2-hour mark, it is time to check on the ribs. You should be able to see the bones beginning to pull away from the meat. Flip the ribs over to the meat side and smoke for 1 more hour. This final hour will result in the color and caramelization we are aiming for and get us up to that internal temperature of 200°F.

7. Remove the ribs from the smoker and immediately brush both sides with the pickle glaze. BE GENTLE! We don't want to disturb that beautiful color and crust we worked so hard for!

CHEAT SHEET

- To set my kettle-style grill up as a smoker, I like to use the minion method for my charcoal: Place a pile of unlit charcoal on half of the grill. Place a small amount of hot, pre-lit briquettes on top of that pile. The lit coals will slowly ignite the unlit pile, resulting in a consistent and steady temperature. Add flavored wood chips such as apple, oak, or hickory to give some flavorful smoke to the meat.

- MUSTARD IS A BINDER! A binder is used to help the seasoning adhere to the meat. Think of it as a glue for the dry rub. The mustard will evaporate during cooking and impart no flavor to the meat. You can also use a neutral oil, mayonnaise, or hot sauce.

PORK BELLY BURNT ENDS

SERVES 12

Of all the ways to prepare and serve pork belly, this is my favorite! Cubing the slab of pork belly prior to cooking allows for all sides to be coated with rub and absorb smoke during the first portion of the cook. This process is very similar to brisket burnt ends, but the additional fat in pork belly results in a very different, equally tasty bite.

1 skinless pork belly

2 tablespoons yellow mustard

5 tablespoons Sweet and Spicy Pork Rub (page 150)

2 cups Classic Sweet BBQ Sauce (page 147)

2 tablespoons honey

2 tablespoons brown sugar

5 tablespoons butter

1. Preheat your smoker to 275°F. I recommend apple or hickory for this cook because it provides a medium smoke that is not too overpowering.

2. Slice then cube the pork belly into 1 x 1-inch pieces. Place the cubes into a bowl and fully coat with a thin layer of yellow mustard. Sprinkle with rub until all pieces have the rub on them.

3. Place the pork belly on the smoker with the fat side up. This portion of the cook will take about 2 hours.

4. When the pork belly reaches 190°F internally, place the pork belly cubes in a half-size aluminum pan, add the BBQ sauce, honey, brown sugar, and remaining rub, and toss to combine, then top with the cubes of butter.

5. Return the pan to the smoker and cook uncovered for 1 hour more, or until the mixture has caramelized and reduced.

6. Remove from the smoker and cool for 10 to 20 minutes to avoid burning the roof of your mouth!

CHEAT SHEET

Arrange the seasoned pork belly cubes on a smoker rack, leaving space between each piece for smoke circulation. This will make it easier to put them on the smoker and take them off.

DRY-RUBBED PORK TENDERLOIN

SERVES 4

I'm a creature of habit—once I find something I like, I usually stick to it. For example, I have the same brand and style T-shirt in eighteen different colors! I can be the same way with my grill. Steak and chicken are pretty common themes in my backyard. If it isn't broke, don't fix it! However, if I need a little push of inspiration, there are few things more delicious than a perfectly seasoned and grilled pork tenderloin. For this recipe, I always opt for a charcoal grill. You can use a gas grill, but that chargrilled flavor is like that one great shot during an otherwise underwhelming round of golf. It always brings me back for more.

1 tablespoon brown sugar

1 tablespoon garlic powder

1 tablespoon chili powder

1 tablespoon kosher salt

1 tablespoon freshly ground black pepper

1 teaspoon smoked paprika

1 teaspoon red pepper flakes

One 1- to 1½-pound pork tenderloin

1. Preheat your grill to high heat.

2. While the grill is heating, mix the brown sugar, garlic powder, chili powder, salt, pepper, smoked paprika, and red pepper flakes in a small bowl to create a spice rub. Pat the tenderloin dry with a paper towel and sprinkle the rub over the meat. Let the meat sit at room temperature for about 20 minutes to allow the rub to "sweat" into the meat.

3. When the grill reaches high heat, place the tenderloin on the grill, close the lid, and cook for 5 minutes. Rotate the tenderloin 45 degrees, close the lid again, and cook for another 5 minutes. Flip and repeat this process. Closing the lid cooks the inside of the pork, while rotating it creates a crosshatch pattern and crust to seal in the juices.

4. Once your pork reaches an internal temperature of 140°F, remove it from the grill, cover loosely with a piece of foil, and let rest for about 15 minutes. During this time the internal temperature will rise 5 to 8 degrees while the tenderloin stays perfectly moist.

CHEAT SHEET

- Use a sharp knife to trim excess fat or silver skin from the surface of the pork tenderloin. This will help the dry rub penetrate the meat and ensure even cooking.

- After seasoning meat, I always allow it to sit out at room temperature for 20 to 30 minutes. This allows the seasoning to really marry and absorb into the meat.

GRILLED PORK STEAKS

SERVES 4

Some of my favorite cuts of meat tend to be some of the most underrated. Pork steak falls into that category. Pork steaks aren't always readily available in stores, but any butcher could cut them for you. They are cut from the Boston butt, which is commonly used to make pulled pork and can be smoked low and slow or grilled hot and fast. The beautiful part is that regardless of the method you choose, they are equally delicious! These steaks are seasoned simply and finished with a tangy, spicy basting liquid that will keep them tender and juicy.

For the Pork:

Four ¾-inch pork steaks

Kosher salt and freshly ground black pepper

Granulated garlic

Onion powder

1. Preheat your grill to medium heat. For that chargrilled flavor, I prefer to use a charcoal grill, but a gas grill will work, too.

2. Season the pork steaks with salt, pepper, granulated garlic, and onion powder. I don't give an exact amount for these four seasonings, because some people like more pepper

For the Basting Liquid:

2 cups apple cider vinegar

½ teaspoon salt

1 tablespoon light brown sugar

½ teaspoon freshly ground black pepper

¼ teaspoon cayenne pepper

¼ teaspoon red pepper flakes

or just a little bit of garlic, for example, so use your own personal judgment.

3. Prepare the basting liquid: Combine all the ingredients in a small pot, place over medium-low heat, and whisk until thoroughly combined. Bring to a simmer and simmer for 5 minutes, or until the brown sugar dissolves.

4. When the grill is ready, place the pork steaks on direct heat. Cook, flipping every 30 to 45 seconds. After each flip, baste. Avoid brushing the pork steaks—instead, drizzle or pat the basting liquid to not disturb the seasoning and crust that will develop. I always make sure I have a section of the grill available as a "safe zone" in case of flare-ups—pork steaks come from the section of a pig called the Boston butt, commonly used for pulled pork, which has a lot of fat, so fat flare-ups are a possibility.

5. Continue the flip/baste method for 15 minutes, until an internal temperature of 140°F is reached. I make sure to cook over medium heat for the duration, as anything too high will likely dry out the pork.

6. Remove the pork steaks from the grill and let rest for 10 to 15 minutes to reach an internal temperature of 145°F.

AL PASTOR-STYLE PULLED PORK

SERVES 15 TO 18

Tacos al pastor is a staple in Mexico. Tender pork, traditionally the loin, is marinated in a spicy and savory marinade and served in a tortilla of choice with a splash of citrus and a palate-cooling tomato salsa. My boys, Aidric and Nash, LOVE tacos. Even though they're only nine and ten, they enjoy some spice and almost look at it as a challenge. My goal with this recipe was to create a pastor-style taco with the perfect balance of heat and sweet that the whole family could enjoy. Salt from the seasoning and marinade, fat from the Boston butt, and acid from the citrus—that first bite will hit every taste bud on the flavor spectrum.

1 cup white vinegar

½ cup water

½ cup pineapple juice

6 tablespoons achiote paste

¼ cup chili powder

¼ cup ground cumin

¼ cup garlic powder

¼ cup kosher salt

2 tablespoons freshly ground black pepper

One 8-pound bone-in Boston butt

½ cup apple juice

1. Preheat your grill or smoker for indirect heat at 300°F.

2. Make the marinade: Combine the vinegar, water, pineapple juice, achiote paste, chili powder, cumin, garlic powder, salt, and pepper in a small bowl and whisk until fully incorporated.

3. Place the pork in a full-size (21 x 13-inch) aluminum pan, then pour the marinade over it, making sure it coats the entire pork butt (it does not need to be submerged).

4. Cover the pan with aluminum foil and let the pork marinate in the refrigerator for at least a few hours.

5. Remove the pork from the marinade, place it on the grill, and cook for 3 to 4 hours, until it reaches an internal temperature of 165°F. We are using the same cooking method as the Groark Boys Pulled Pork recipe (page 28), simply different flavors.

6. Place the pork in a disposable foil half pan (9 x 13 inches), add the apple juice, and cover tightly with a sheet of foil. Place the pan on the grill and continue cooking until the pork reaches an internal temperature of 203°F, about 2 more hours.

7. Remove the pork from the grill and rest in a cooler or Cambro for at least 3 hours.

8. Shred the meat, making sure to mix in all the juices in the pan. To serve, place on your choice of tostados or tortillas and top with your choice of toppings, such as pineapple chunks, salsa, cilantro, and onion.

"BRISKET"-STYLE PORK BELLY

SERVES 8

Traditionally, pork belly is cured, slow smoked, and sliced into bacon. It is a very tedious and long process that requires a great deal of patience. To save time and simplify the cook, I came up with this recipe by cooking the pork belly like a brisket. This method not only makes things quicker and easier, it creates a ton of different presentation and serving options for the finished product. Slice thick with your favorite BBQ sauce and sides for a melt-in-your-mouth bite, or pan-sear to caramelize both sides for that perfect crust and serve in a sandwich topped with some Smack Slaw (page 156). No matter how you decide to serve it, you'll get that classic pork belly taste without the hassle of curing and slow-smoking.

One 2-pound boneless, skinless pork belly

Sweet and Spicy Pork Rub (page 150)

1. Preheat your smoker to 275°F.

2. To prep the pork belly, trim off excess silver skin and slice off any uneven edges so you are left with an even rectangle piece of meat. This will ensure that the pork belly cooks evenly. Season the pork belly liberally with the rub.

3. Place in the smoker and cook for 3 hours, or until the pork reaches an internal temperature of 170°F. At this stage, the pork belly will be a beautiful mahogany color with some bark developed. Remove from the smoker, wrap in pink butcher paper, and continue to cook at 275°F until it reaches an internal temperature of 205°F, about 1 more hour.

4. Rest for 30 minutes, slice, and serve!

BEEF

Grilling and smoking beef is an art, a tradition that has earned a royal status in the world of barbecue and in backyards everywhere. It's no coincidence that beef is hailed as the "king of BBQ." I will teach you a tender and smoky backyard brisket that any aspiring pitmaster can conquer. It's a labor of love that is well worth the time and commitment. In this section, you'll find a wide variety of flavors—from the southwestern flair of grilled steak fajitas to the rich, melt-in-your-mouth smoked beef plate ribs, commonly referred to as dino bones. Beef knows no bounds, and every bite represents the work, dedication, and passion that goes into creating amazing BBQ!

- Grilled Steak Fajitas
- Next-Level Grilled Filet Mignon Sandwich with Gorgonzola Crema and Blueberry Sauce
- Smoked Dino Ribs
- Cheddar and Mozzarella–Stuffed Smoked Burgers
- Smoked Tri-Tip with Chimichurri Sauce
- Kalbi-Style Korean BBQ Short Ribs
- Chuck Roast Burnt Ends
- Reverse-Seared Bone-in Ribeye Steak
- Smoked Beef Short Ribs
- Perfectly Smoked Backyard Brisket

GRILLED STEAK FAJITAS

SERVES 4

My older sister was a waitress at a popular food establishment not far from our hometown, Erial, New Jersey, very well-known for a viral jingle that had everyone singing, "I want my baby back, baby back, baby back, ribs!" Throughout the fall and winter, I would meet a couple friends there on Sunday or Monday nights to watch the week's prime-time NFL matchup, but it wasn't the ribs I would order. My meal of choice was always the fajitas. I can still remember the sweet harmony of that sizzle as my eyes locked in on that trail of steam following behind the server.

Over the years, re-creating those nights at home has been a trip down memory lane. Isn't that a big part of what food should do? This recipe takes me right back to that moment and reminds me of great times—and delicious fajitas—shared with friends and family.

1 teaspoon chili powder

1 teaspoon paprika

1 teaspoon ground cumin

Kosher salt and freshly cracked black pepper to taste

1 pound flank steak

1 red bell pepper, sliced

1 green bell pepper, sliced

1 yellow onion, sliced

2 cloves garlic, minced

1 tablespoon extra virgin olive oil

4 to 8 flour tortillas

1. Preheat your grill to high heat.

2. Mix the chili powder, paprika, cumin, salt, and pepper in a small bowl. Rub the mixture onto the flank steak.

3. Set the steak on the grill and cook for 5 minutes on each side, or until the internal temperature reaches 130°F for medium-rare. After that initial 10 minutes, check the internal temperature with a probe, and if not quite there yet, cook for another couple minutes per side.

4. While the steak is on the grill, mix the bell peppers, onion, garlic, and oil in a large bowl. Season with salt and pepper. Place the vegetable mixture in a grill basket, place on the grill, and cook until tender and slightly charred, 5 to 7 minutes.

5. Once the steak reaches 130°F, remove it from the grill and let rest on a cutting board for 10 minutes. Remember, the steak will continue to rise in temperature about another 5 degrees.

6. Thinly slice the steak against the grain. Serve the sliced steak and grilled vegetables on warm flour tortillas. If desired, add your favorite toppings, such as guacamole, sour cream, and shredded cheese.

CHEAT SHEET

- Skirt steak can be substituted for the flank steak, as it takes very well to a marinade and is incredibly tender and flavorful.

- Regardless of the cut used, be sure to slice the steak against the grain.

NEXT-LEVEL GRILLED FILET MIGNON SANDWICH WITH GORGONZOLA CREMA AND BLUEBERRY SAUCE

SERVES 2

Let me set the stage. Gordon Ramsay, *Next Level Chef*, Season 2, Episode 3, Sandwich Challenge! I'm in the top kitchen, which means I get first choice of ingredients and equipment Michelin star chefs dream of! 3–2–1, the platform drops, and the mad rush ensues. I grab a filet mignon, the Rolls-Royce of steak, blue cheese, and artichokes, and I make a chili aioli. Gordon Ramsay called it one of the tastiest sandwiches of the day and Nyesha Arrington said the flavors were impeccable. Was it the sandwich I envisioned? No! However, when I'm home, I get to use the ingredients I would have wished for to build my perfect sandwich. I am drawing inspiration from that day to bring you a simple yet delicious steak sandwich that I know would have won that challenge!

For the Sandwiches:

Two 6- to 8-ounce filet mignons, about ½ pound each

1 tablespoon extra virgin olive oil

Kosher salt and freshly cracked black pepper

4 slices sourdough bread

1 bunch arugula

1 red onion, sliced into rounds

For the Gorgonzola Crema:

¾ cup Gorgonzola cheese

⅓ cup sour cream

2 tablespoons apple cider vinegar

Lemon zest (optional)

1. Heat a large cast-iron pan or grill over medium-high heat.

2. Coat the filets with oil and season all over with salt and pepper. Set aside.

3. Make the Gorgonzola crema: In a small bowl, combine the cheese, sour cream, vinegar, and lemon zest (if using). Season with salt and pepper and mix until fully combined. Set aside.

4. Make the blueberry sauce: In a large sauté pan, melt ½ tablespoon of the butter with the oil over medium heat. Add the garlic and rosemary and cook for 2 minutes.

5. Add the honey, salt, pepper, and blueberries, then stir in the vinegar. Reduce the heat to low and simmer for 5 minutes or so, until the blueberries begin to soften and the sauce begins to reduce.

6. Add the remaining ½ tablespoon butter and cook for another 3 minutes. Remove from the heat.

Kosher salt and freshly cracked black pepper

For the Blueberry Sauce:

1 tablespoon butter

1 tablespoon extra virgin olive oil

1 teaspoon minced garlic

1 tablespoon minced fresh rosemary

1 tablespoon honey

⅛ teaspoon kosher salt

¼ teaspoon freshly ground black pepper

1 cup fresh blueberries

2 tablespoons balsamic vinegar

7. Set the steak on the cast-iron pan or grill and cook for 4 to 5 minutes on each side, until the internal temperature reaches 135°F for medium-rare. For better texture and color, I like to "roll" the filet over the grill on all sides for an extra minute.

8. Remove from the heat and let rest on a cutting board for 5 minutes.

9. Time to build the sandwiches! Toast the sourdough bread to your desired level.

10. Spread the Gorgonzola crema on BOTH slices of bread. Slice the rested filet mignon steak against the grain into thin strips and place on top of the crema.

11. Top the steak with a heaping tablespoon of blueberry sauce and finish with red onions and arugula. Slice the sandwiches in half and enjoy.

SMOKED DINO RIBS

SERVES 4 TO 6

Beef plate ribs, also known as "dino bones," are an absolute treat and deliver everything that you love about brisket, but with a handle! I remember my first time biting into a beef rib like I remember my first kiss. I was at Myron Mixon's BBQ Cooking School in Unadilla, Georgia, and the first night there we were treated to a southern BBQ dinner featuring all of Myron's award-winning meats and sides. I went right for that beef rib. It was a meaty, fatty, juicy, and tender bite of beef that I will never forget. There are many ways to smoke beef plate ribs, and this is not only my favorite but one you will find easy and extremely memorable from the very first bite.

4 to 5½ pounds beef plate ribs (3 to 4 bones)

2 tablespoons yellow mustard

6 tablespoons RubCity Groark Boys BBQ for Beef Rub (or equal parts kosher salt and freshly cracked black pepper)

1. Preheat your smoker to 275°F. I go for a traditional Texas-style beef rib, so I add a couple chunks of oakwood to my smoker. Don't overdo it, because too much smoke can ruin the meat.

2. To prep the ribs, remove the layer of fat and silver skin from on top of the ribs—this layer can be very unpleasant and will not render, so don't skip this step! Unlike prepping pork ribs, you don't need to do anything to the membrane on the bone side of the ribs. Keeping the membrane on will help keep the ribs together.

3. Lightly coat the beef ribs with the mustard and season with the rub.

4. Place the seasoned ribs on the smoker, close the lid, and do not touch for 3 hours.

5. At that point, the internal temperature of the beef ribs will be hovering around 160°F internal and the bark should be a beautiful mahogany color. It will be tempting to wrap the ribs in foil or butcher paper at this point, but doing so can impact that bark, so I keep the ribs unwrapped straight through.

6. It will take another 3 to 4 hours to reach that 205°F

internal temperature and get that beautiful bark we all want. When you're there (6 to 7 hours total), pull the ribs off the smoker.

7. Some people like to rest their beef ribs in a cooler for an hour or more, but I have found that, unlike brisket and pork butt, beef ribs can be served immediately.

CHEAT SHEET

- When I make beef ribs, I really want the quality of the meat to shine through, so I go very simple on the seasoning.

- It's important to trim any excess fat from the surface of the ribs but leave a thin layer to help keep the meat moist during smoking. Removing excess fat can help the smoke penetrate the meat more effectively.

CHEDDAR AND MOZZARELLA-STUFFED SMOKED BURGERS

SERVES 4

Thanks to a mix of cherry and oakwood smoke, these burgers have a deliciously mild smoky taste and a beautiful mahogany color. This recipe pushes the flavor a step further by stuffing these juicy burgers with a gooey combination of cheddar and mozzarella cheese. So, let's fire up the smoker and get ready to indulge!

1 pound 80/20 ground beef

4 slices cheddar cheese

4 slices mozzarella cheese

Kosher salt and freshly cracked black pepper

4 hamburger buns

Optional toppings: lettuce, tomato, onion, pickles, ketchup, mustard, mayonnaise

1. Preheat your smoker to 300°F with a mixture of cherry- and oakwood.

2. Divide the ground beef into 4 equal portions. Flatten each portion into a thin patty. Trim the cheddar and mozzarella cheese slices into 4 square pieces to fit nicely in the center of the patties. Place 2 slices of cheddar and 2 slices of mozzarella directly in the center of 2 of the patties, leaving about an inch of beef around the edges.

3. Place the remaining 2 patties on top of the cheese-topped patties. Press the edges together firmly to seal the cheese inside. Make sure the edges are completely sealed to prevent leakage. Season the stuffed burgers with salt and pepper on both sides.

4. Place the stuffed burgers on the smoker and cook for 30 minutes. Resist the temptation to open the lid during this time so you maintain a consistent temperature.

5. After 30 minutes, check the internal temperature of the burgers using an instant-read meat thermometer. For medium doneness, the burgers should reach an internal temperature of 145°F. Adjust the cooking time accordingly if you prefer your burgers more or less well done.

6. Remove the burgers from the smoker and let them rest. Meanwhile, toast the hamburger buns.

7. Place each smoked burger on a toasted bun. Add your favorite toppings. Serve the burgers immediately and prepare for a flavor explosion!

CHEAT SHEET

- Be sure the stuffed burgers are well sealed to prevent the cheese from leaking out as they smoke.

- Get creative with your toppings. Add your favorite condiments, vegetables, or cheeses to enhance the flavor profile.

SMOKED TRI-TIP WITH CHIMICHURRI SAUCE

SERVES 4 TO 6

Tri-tip is a cut of beef I never knew existed until my journey on social media started to take shape. Originally called the Santa Maria steak thanks to the California town that made it popular, the tri-tip is a cut from the bottom sirloin. As I connected with more and more people in the food community online, I quickly realized this was a cut of steak I had to master.

The triangular-shaped cut boasts so much flavor and is extremely tender—as long as it's not overcooked and sliced correctly. The latter can be a little tricky. The muscle grains in the tri-tip

change direction, so to cut against the grain, you will have to rotate halfway through when slicing. By smoking indirect, we are going to make sure our internal temperature is a perfect medium-rare and then slice against the grain for a perfectly cooked and tender tri-tip. Served with a traditional chimichurri sauce, this is a recipe that I know will do my California friends proud!

For the Tri-Tip:

One 2- to 3-pound tri-tip roast

2 tablespoons extra virgin olive oil

Kosher salt and freshly cracked black pepper

For the Chimichurri:

1 cup chopped fresh parsley

½ cup chopped fresh cilantro

4 cloves garlic, minced

1 teaspoon dried oregano

1 teaspoon red pepper flakes (optional)

2 tablespoons red wine vinegar

Kosher salt and freshly cracked black pepper to taste

½ cup extra virgin olive oil

1. Preheat your smoker to 275°F with your choice of wood. For beef, I like to use oak because it provides a perfect smoky flavor without overpowering the meat.

2. Rub the tri-tip with the oil and season with salt and pepper. Place the seasoned tri-tip on the smoker and cook for 1 to 1½ hours, until it reaches an internal temperature of 125°F.

3. While the tri-tip smokes, prepare the chimichurri. In a small bowl, mix the parsley, cilantro, garlic, oregano, red pepper flakes (if using), vinegar, salt, pepper, and oil and set aside.

4. Once the tri-tip reaches 125°F, remove it from the smoker and heat a large cast-iron skillet over high heat. Place the smoked tri-tip on the pan and sear for 2 minutes per side to develop a crust and bring the internal temperature up to 130°F to 135°F for medium-rare to medium. I also like to finish directly over some ripping-hot charcoal. Remove and rest on a cutting board for 10 minutes.

5. Slice the rested tri-tip against the grain into thin strips. Serve with the chimichurri sauce on the side.

CHEAT SHEET

The grain of the meat in a tri-tip changes directions halfway through the cut, so be sure to pay attention while slicing and rotate the meat when needed to continue slicing against the grain.

KALBI-STYLE KOREAN BBQ SHORT RIBS

SERVES 4 TO 6

My first time making Korean BBQ short ribs was at my brother's house in Washington Township, New Jersey, at a summer pool party. We needed something fast and delicious, so I ran to the store and happened to see some beautifully marbled flanken short ribs. Korean short ribs, flanken ribs, kalbi-style ribs, call them what you want, but they quickly became one of my favorite things to throw on the grill! They take no time to make and are even more delicious when paired with this easy-to-make sweet and savory marinade. This recipe is perfect for a summer cookout or anytime you crave the irresistible combination of sweet, savory, and smoky goodness.

For the Marinade:

½ cup soy sauce

½ cup brown sugar

¼ cup sake or rice wine

¼ cup honey

4 cloves garlic, minced

2 tablespoons sesame oil

2 tablespoons sesame seeds

1 tablespoon grated fresh ginger

1 tablespoon gochujang (Korean chili paste)

2 green onions, sliced

For the Ribs:

2 pounds Korean-style beef short ribs

Kosher salt and freshly cracked black pepper

1. Make the marinade: Whisk the soy sauce, brown sugar, sake, honey, garlic, oil, sesame seeds, ginger, gochujang, and green onions in a large bowl.

2. Season the ribs with salt and pepper. Put the seasoned ribs in the marinade bowl and toss them to coat them evenly. Cover with plastic wrap and refrigerate for at least 8 hours or overnight.

3. Preheat your grill to medium-high heat. Take the short ribs out of the marinade and discard the remaining marinade.

4. Place the short ribs on the grill and cook for 3 to 4 minutes per side. Because the ribs are very thin, this short amount of time is perfect for a medium-cooked rib. If you prefer yours more well done, add a couple minutes. Be careful to check often and flip as needed. You want the ribs to caramelize, not burn.

5. Remove from the grill and serve as whole ribs or cut them into individual ribs between the bones.

CHEAT SHEET

For maximum flavor, I prep these the night before and marinate them overnight in the refrigerator to allow the flavors to penetrate the meat fully.

CHUCK ROAST BURNT ENDS

SERVES 4 TO 6

This recipe turned out to be one of my first truly viral videos on TikTok, way back in 2018. Burnt ends are made from the point of a whole packer brisket. However, the term has more recently been applied to several cuts of meat (pork belly, pork butt, chuck roast) and cooked with a very similar method. You may have also heard these called poor man's burnt ends because it's chuck roast instead of brisket. While both cuts of meat are comparable in terms of price per pound, for brisket you typically have to purchase a whole brisket (15+ pounds), while with chuck you can use a smaller 3-pound roast. Rich or poor, this recipe takes a boring chuck roast and transforms it into tender and delectable cubes of beef candy. Instead of my rub, you could use a simple mix of kosher salt, black pepper, and garlic powder.

One 3-pound chuck roast

1 tablespoon yellow mustard

2 tablespoons RubCity Groark Boys BBQ for Beef Rub or another rub

½ cup Classic Sweet BBQ Sauce (page 147)

½ cup dark brown sugar

1. Preheat your smoker to 275°F. I like to use oak or hickory for my beef recipes, and they both go perfectly with chuck roast.

2. Slather your chuck roast with the mustard as a binder and season with the rub.

3. Time to smoke the meat! Place the chuck roast on the smoker and cook until it reaches an internal temperature of 165°F. For a 3-pound chuck roast, this should take about 4 hours, but remember, every piece of meat is different!

4. Time to wrap! Remove the chuck roast from the smoker and wrap in butcher paper or foil. Place back on the smoker and cook until it reaches an internal temperature of 200°F, about 1 hour.

5. Remove the wrapped chuck roast from the smoker, cut into 1-inch cubes, and transfer to a foil baking pan. Add the BBQ sauce and sprinkle with the brown sugar. Toss gently to coat all the pieces.

6. Place the pan on the grill and cover with a lid or foil. Cook for an additional 2 hours, or until the sauce mixture is bubbling and the cubed chuck is break-apart tender.

7. Remove the lid and close the smoker for a final 15 to 20 minutes. This helps to really set the sauce and make sure everything is fully incorporated. Serve as a main course or on potato buns with pickles or slaw.

CHEAT SHEET

- While chuck roast has some natural fat, you may want to trim excess fat from the surface of the meat. Leaving a thin layer of fat will add flavor and moisture, but too much fat can result in greasy burnt ends.

- You can also use this method with other cuts of beef, such as brisket or pork shoulder.

REVERSE-SEARED BONE-IN RIBEYE STEAK

SERVES 2 TO 3

When I discovered the reverse-sear method, it took my steak game to the next level. Cooking this reverse-seared bone-in ribeye over charcoal combines the best of both worlds: the slow, gentle heat of indirect cooking and the intense, flavor-packed sear that only charcoal can provide. As the coals smolder and ignite, we infuse the steak with a smoky essence that pairs perfectly and complements a succulent and fatty ribeye steak. By starting with low heat and gradually bringing the steak up to your ideal internal temperature, followed by a sizzling sear to create an unparalleled crust, you'll end up with a piece of meat that is moist, juicy, and packed with phenomenal flavor.

1 bone-in ribeye steak (about 2 pounds)

2 tablespoons RubCity Groark Boys BBQ for Beef Rub (or equal parts kosher salt and freshly ground black pepper

1. Preheat your grill to two-zone cooking at 300°F.

2. Pat the ribeye steak dry with paper towels to remove excess moisture. Season the steak on all sides with the rub. Place on a tray and allow the steak to sweat at room temperature for 15 to 20 minutes for the seasoning to penetrate the meat.

3. Once the grill is preheated, place the steak on the side of the grill without direct heat (the indirect zone).

4. Monitor the internal temperature of the steak using an instant-read meat thermometer. Cook the steak until it reaches an internal temperature of about 120°F for medium-rare. This slow cooking process will help evenly cook the steak and develop a nice crust. Remove the steak and set the grill to high heat.

5. Set the steak aside temporarily. Place the steak directly over the high heat and sear each side for 1 to 2 minutes, to an internal temperature of 130°F.

6. Transfer the steak to a cutting board and tent it loosely with aluminum foil. Let it rest for about 10 minutes to allow the juices to redistribute. This resting period will result in a more tender and flavorful steak. Slice the steak and serve immediately.

CHEAT SHEET

Cooking time may vary depending on the thickness of the steak and the grill temperature, so it's important to monitor the internal temperature of the steak using an instant-read meat thermometer to achieve your desired level of doneness. Adjust the cooking time accordingly.

SMOKED BEEF SHORT RIBS

SERVES 4 TO 6

Known for their rich flavor and tender meat, smoked beef short ribs are a true barbecue delicacy. Slow-smoking these beefy cuts over oakwood imparts a smokiness that beautifully complements the robust beef flavor. With the right technique and a little patience, the result is perfectly smoked beef short ribs. Fire up your smoker, grab some wood, and get started!

4 beef short ribs, bone-in (3 to 4 pounds total)

Salt and freshly ground black pepper

RubCity Groark Boys BBQ for Beef Rub or another beef dry rub (optional)

1. Preheat your smoker to 250°F to 275°F.

2. Trim excess fat from the beef short ribs, leaving a thin layer for flavor and moisture. Season the ribs generously with salt and pepper. For extra flavor, apply the rub, ensuring that the ribs are evenly coated. Let the ribs sit at room temperature while the smoker preheats, about 20 minutes.

3. Place soaked oakwood chunks or chips directly onto the charcoal or in the smoker's wood chip box. Oak is an excellent choice for smoking beef, as it imparts a robust flavor. Once the smoker has reached temperature, arrange the short ribs on the smoker grates, bone-side down. Close the smoker's lid to maintain a consistent temperature.

4. Smoke the short ribs for 4 to 5 hours, depending on their thickness and desired tenderness. Maintain the smoker's temperature between 250°F and 275°F throughout the smoking process. For optimal tenderness, aim for an internal temperature of 195°F to 203°F. Always focus more on internal temperature over time, as every piece of meat and smoker is different. The meat should be tender and easily pull away from the bone.

5. For even more tenderness, you can wrap the short ribs in aluminum foil once they reach an internal temperature of around 160°F to 165°F. This technique, known as the

"Texas crutch," helps accelerate the cooking process and lock in moisture. However, if you prefer a firmer bark, like I do, you can skip this step and cook straight through.

6. Once the short ribs have reached your desired tenderness, remove them from the smoker. Place them in an aluminum half pan, wrap loosely in foil, and set aside for about 30 minutes to allow the juices to redistribute. This resting period helps ensure a moist and flavorful result. After resting, unwrap the ribs and serve immediately.

CHEAT SHEET

- Select high-quality beef short ribs with good marbling for the best flavor and tenderness.

- Smoking short ribs is a slow process, so be patient and resist the temptation to rush. Low and slow cooking allows the connective tissues to break down, resulting in tender meat.

- Only open the smoker when necessary, such as to check the temperature or wrap the ribs if desired. Each time you open the smoker, heat and smoke escape, which can impact the cooking time and smoke flavor.

- To help keep the meat moist and enhance flavor, consider using a spray bottle filled with water or apple juice to periodically spritz the short ribs while smoking.

- Resting the short ribs after smoking is crucial. This allows the juices to redistribute, resulting in more tender and succulent meat.

PERFECTLY SMOKED BACKYARD BRISKET

SERVES 15 TO 20

There is something magical about the time spent smoking brisket in the comfort of your own backyard. I have made plenty of mistakes while learning how to cook a great brisket, and trust me when I say, I still do. However, this is the method I learned from Myron Mixon's BBQ Cooking School, and it is the one I have been the most consistent using. "Hot and fast" is the method, which means we are smoking at a higher temperature than the traditional low and slow. This is achievable using a trusty kettle grill or a convenient pellet smoker—the result will be the same. With a little know-how, patience, and some helpful tips, you will have a method you can go back to time and time again.

One 15- to 17-pound whole beef brisket, packer-cut (with both the point and flat sections)

2 tablespoons yellow mustard

2 cups RubCity Texas Hat Hanger BBQ Rub and Seasoning (or 1 cup kosher salt and 1 cup freshly ground black pepper)

2 cups beef broth

1. Trim excess fat from the brisket, leaving about ¼ inch for flavor and moisture. Trim off any loose or hanging pieces to ensure even cooking and prevent any pieces from burning and drying out.

2. Slather your brisket with the mustard as a binder and season with the rub. Make sure the brisket is evenly coated on all sides.

3. If you're using a kettle grill: Set up your grill for indirect heat by placing an aluminum drip pan in the center and arranging charcoal briquettes on either side. Add a handful of wood chunks (I like to use hickory or oak) on top of the charcoal to create smoke. Preheat the grill to about 300°F. If you're using a pellet smoker: Fill the hopper with your preferred wood pellets. Preheat the smoker to 300°F.

4. Place the seasoned brisket in the center of the grill or smoker grate. Close the lid and let the magic happen.

5. Maintain a consistent smoking temperature of 300°F throughout the cooking process. This slightly higher temperature will help render the fat and speed up the cooking time.

6. When the brisket probes at 165°F and has beautiful dark mahogany bark, you are ready to wrap. If you feel the bark needs more time, you can allow it to go to 175°F internal.

7. Place your brisket in a full-size disposable aluminum pan and set it on a rack to elevate it. Pour the beef broth in the bottom and wrap the pan in aluminum foil tightly to seal. This helps retain moisture and speeds up the cooking process.

8. Return the wrapped brisket to the grill or smoker and continue cooking until it reaches an internal temperature of to 205°F.

9. Remove the brisket from the grill or smoker, keeping it wrapped, and let it rest in a prepared cooler or Cambro warming box for at least 3 hours. Resting allows the juices to redistribute, resulting in a tender and juicy brisket.

10. Put on heat-resistant gloves or mitts and carefully unwrap the brisket. Transfer it to a cutting board.

11. Slice the brisket against the grain, starting from the flat section and working toward the point. Aim for slices that are ¼ to ½ inch thick.

12. Serve with your favorite barbecue sauce, pickles, onions, or other traditional accompaniments.

CHEAT SHEET

- Wrapping the brisket in foil or butcher paper helps speed up the cooking process and keeps the meat moist. Foil provides a more tender result, while butcher paper creates a great bark. Choose the method that suits your preference.

- Maintain a steady smoker temperature of 300°F throughout the cooking process to achieve consistent results.

- Use an instant-read meat thermometer to monitor the internal temperature. The brisket is done when it reaches a temperature of 195°F to 203°F and the meat probes tenderly.

- Allow the brisket to rest for at least 3 hours after cooking. This resting period allows the juices to redistribute, resulting in a more succulent and flavorful final product.

- Cutting against the grain ensures each slice is tender and easy to chew. Pay attention to the natural grain lines of the meat and adjust your slicing accordingly.

CHICKEN

Chicken is such a versatile protein. I consider it a blank canvas whose flavor will not truly take flight until it is on the grill or in the smoker. My goal here is to express the myriad ways chicken can be transformed into a smoky and succulent appetizer or main dish, from the tender smokiness of BBQ Spatchcock Chicken to a Grilled Romaine Chicken Caesar. Beer Can Chicken, zesty Lemon and Herb Marinated Chicken Thighs, and my addictive Pickle-Glazed Chicken Wings are a few of my favorites. BBQ Bacon-Wrapped Drumsticks seemed impossible to me at first, but through a lot of trial and error, I created a method that marries perfectly juicy chicken and smoky bacon. Chicken is the canvas, flavor is the masterpiece, and you are the artist with endless grilling and smoking adventures ahead of you.

- Smoked BBQ Spatchcock Chicken
- Grilled Romaine Chicken Caesar Salad
- Applewood Smoked Beer Can Chicken
- Lemon and Herb Marinated Chicken Thighs
- Smoked Pickle-Glazed Chicken Wings
- BBQ Peach-Glazed Chicken Kabobs
- Jerk Marinated Chicken Thighs
- Honey-Mustard Glazed Wings
- Smoked BBQ Bacon-Wrapped Drumsticks

SMOKED BBQ SPATCHCOCK CHICKEN

SERVES 4 TO 6

There are so many ways to cook a whole chicken, but in my humble opinion, a spatchcock chicken reigns supreme. Not only does it present beautifully, but because the bird is flattened and the backbone is removed, it cooks faster and more evenly than any other method. In my daily life as a teacher, it's important I have as many "tools in my toolbelt" as possible to deal with any situation. Short on time? Spatchcock. Impress your friends? Spatchcock. Show off your butchering skills? Spatchcock. It really is that easy!

1 whole chicken

2 tablespoons Poultry Rub
(page 151)

½ cup your favorite BBQ sauce

1. Preheat your smoker to 275°F.

2. Place the chicken on a large cutting board and pat dry with paper towels. Arrange the chicken breast-side down on the cutting board with the neck facing toward you. Using kitchen shears, cut along one side of the chicken's spine, separating it from the ribs. Cut as close to the spine as you can. Repeat on the other side of the spine. If you are having difficulty getting through the bird, rotate it so the tail faces you and cut from the other side. Flip the chicken so the breasts face upward and the legs face outward. Using the palms of your hands, press down along the breastbone. You will likely hear a small crack. This should flatten the chicken completely.

3. Season the spatchcocked chicken with the rub.

4. Place the seasoned chicken in the smoker and cook for 2 hours, or until the internal temperature reaches 160°F.

5. Brush the BBQ sauce over the chicken and continue smoking for 10 minutes, until the sauce has become tacky and caramelized. Remove the chicken from the smoker and rest on a cutting board for 5 to 10 minutes. Butcher the chicken into separate parts (breasts, thighs, legs, and wings) and serve immediately.

CHEAT SHEET

Invest in a pair of high-quality kitchen shears. While it's possible to spatchcock a chicken with a very sharp knife, kitchen shears are safer and more efficient, and they can be used in many other cooking applications.

GRILLED ROMAINE CHICKEN CAESAR SALAD

SERVES 4

My wife, Kristin, is vegetarian, and since I'm someone who—as you probably know by now—primarily cooks meat, this means getting creative. Salads can get a bad rap, but thanks to this recipe, our family celebrates salad nights in the same way many people celebrate Taco Tuesday. Sounds a little silly, but it's true. For a veggie-forward main that's just as satisfying and fun as a meat one, I turned to what I know: grilling! Romaine lettuce can withstand a little bit of char from the grill while maintaining its texture. Perfectly seasoned chargrilled chicken breast finished with a creamy homemade Caesar dressing makes for a most definitely leveled-up salad. For Kristin, I skip the anchovies and substitute her favorite black bean burger for the chicken.

For the Chicken:

4 boneless, skinless chicken breasts

Extra virgin olive oil

Kosher salt and freshly ground black pepper

1 teaspoon garlic powder

1 teaspoon dried basil

1 teaspoon dried oregano

For the Caesar Salad:

4 heads romaine lettuce, halved lengthwise

2 tablespoons extra virgin olive oil

Kosher salt and freshly ground black pepper

1 cup mayonnaise

½ cup sour cream

2 cloves garlic, minced

2 anchovy fillets, minced

2 tablespoons lemon juice

1 teaspoon Dijon mustard

1. Preheat your grill for indirect cooking on high heat.

2. To grill the chicken: Lightly coat the chicken breasts with oil and season with salt, pepper, and the garlic powder, basil, and oregano.

3. Place the seasoned chicken breasts on the preheated grill on high heat and cook for 4 to 5 minutes on each side. Move to the indirect side and cook until the chicken reaches an internal temperature of 165°F. Grill marks should be prominent and the breasts should be firm to the touch with just a slight bounce-back.

4. Remove the chicken from the grill, let rest on a cutting board for 5 minutes, then slice into strips or cut into chunks for plating.

5. In the meantime, brush the lettuce with the oil and rub it with salt and pepper. Place the seasoned lettuce on the direct side of the grill and cook for 2 minutes on each side, or until the lettuce is charred and wilted.

6. Make the dressing: Whisk together the mayonnaise, sour cream, garlic, anchovy fillets, lemon juice, and mustard and season with salt and pepper. It is really that easy!

7. Assemble the salad: Place the grilled lettuce on a serving platter, top with the grilled chicken breasts, and drizzle with the dressing. Serve immediately.

CHEAT SHEET

Grill the romaine lettuce halves cut-side down until lightly charred and just slightly wilted. Be careful not to overcook it so it maintains some crispness.

APPLEWOOD SMOKED BEER CAN CHICKEN

SERVES 4 TO 6

BBQ and beer go hand in hand, so anytime I get a chance to connect the two in a recipe, I take full advantage. Beer can chicken is one of the most well-known alternatives to making BBQ chicken in your backyard. The beer not only acts as a perch for the chicken to "stand" upright on its legs, but the steam it creates within the interior of the chicken helps keep your chicken moist and cook from the inside out. Coated with my all-purpose BBQ dry rub, you will be left with a juicy chicken kissed with a subtle sweet applewood smoke.

One 4- to 5-pound whole chicken

1 teaspoon extra virgin olive oil

2 tablespoons All-Purpose BBQ Rub (page 150)

1 can of your favorite beer (I like to use a lager, as it provides moisture more than flavor)

½ cup BBQ sauce

1. Preheat your smoker to 275°F with applewood. Applewood gives a sweet and subtle smoky flavor.

2. Pat the chicken dry, coat with the oil, and season with the rub.

3. Open the can of beer and pour out—or drink—about one-quarter of the beer. Set the seasoned chicken on top of the beer can, balancing it on its legs and the beer can.

4. Place the chicken perched on the beer can on the preheated smoker and cook for about 2 hours, until it reaches an internal temperature of 160°F. The skin will be a beautiful mahogany and juices will be running clear.

5. Remove the chicken and beer can from the grill and let rest for 5 to 10 minutes, until the chicken is at a finished internal temperature of 165°F (since you're removing the chicken at 160ºF, the carryover cooking during this resting period is key!).

6. Carefully remove the chicken from the beer can. Carve the chicken into pieces and serve.

CHEAT SHEET

A quick search on the interwebs will present you with beer can chicken stands that will hold the can of beer in place and prevent your chicken from tipping over. A minimal investment.

LEMON AND HERB MARINATED CHICKEN THIGHS

SERVES 4 TO 6

Lemon and herb is a classic flavor combination that tastes great on a number of proteins. It works especially well with poultry, so we are making a quick and easy marinade for some chicken thighs. I love the versatility of this marinade because it can be used on any cut of chicken—thighs are my favorite—and is even excellent on pork. The grill will give the thighs in this recipe a nice char, but they'd also taste great pan-seared. Depending on your mood, you can serve these as the star of a complete dinner or slice them up on top of a salad or in a wrap!

½ cup extra virgin olive oil

¼ cup lemon juice

4 cloves garlic, minced

2 tablespoons chopped fresh rosemary

2 tablespoons chopped fresh thyme

2 tablespoons chopped fresh basil

Kosher salt and freshly ground black pepper

8 to 10 boneless, skinless chicken thighs

1. Make the marinade: Whisk together the oil, lemon juice, garlic, rosemary, thyme, and basil in a large bowl. Season with salt and pepper.

2. Add the chicken thighs to the bowl with the marinade and move them around to evenly coat. Cover and refrigerate for at least 30 minutes or up to 2 hours. Alternatively, you can marinate the chicken in a zip-top bag and save yourself some cleanup!

3. Preheat your grill to medium-high heat. Take the chicken thighs out of the marinade and season with a little salt and pepper. Set the chicken thighs on the preheated grill and cook for 10 to 12 minutes, flipping every minute. Serve immediately.

CHEAT SHEET

- **Leftovers:** If you have lots of chicken thighs left over, divide them into smaller portions so you can reheat only what you need later, reducing the risk of food waste. Store in airtight containers or resealable plastic bags. Make sure there's minimal air inside the containers or bags, as air can invite freezer burn or spoilage. Wrapping the chicken in aluminum foil before placing it in the container further preserves moisture. Label the containers or bags with the date you cooked the chicken to help you keep track of its freshness.

- **Refrigeration:** If you plan to eat leftovers within 3 to 4 days, store them in the refrigerator at a temperature of 40°F or below. Place it on the shelves, not in the door, as the door is subject to temperature fluctuations.

- **Freezing:** If you won't be using leftovers within a few days, consider freezing them. Use a freezer-safe container or bag and remove as much air as possible. Store in the freezer at 0°F or lower, where it will keep for 2 to 6 months.

CHEAT SHEET

I have a mason jar of this glaze in my refrigerator
at all times. Kristin and the boys love it, and
it goes well on any protein, even tofu!

SMOKED PICKLE-GLAZED CHICKEN WINGS

SERVES 4 TO 6

Pickle juice is often used as a brine for chicken. A few years ago, I came across a recipe by celebrity chef Michael Symon, who used it in a glaze for pork ribs. My wife and I had some friends over, and it just so happened I was making that rib recipe along with some chicken wings. I had no intention to use the pickle glaze on the chicken, but, as in life, sometimes cooking and recipes can take a turn. The wings were perfectly seasoned and charred, so I finished them with a soft brush of the pickle glaze and this recipe was decided!

1 teaspoon baking powder

1 tablespoon Sweet and Spicy Pork Rub (page 150)

2 pounds chicken wings

1 cup pickle juice

2 cups light brown sugar

1. Preheat your smoker to 300ºF.

2. While the smoker is preheating, prepare the rub mixture and the pickle glaze: In a large bowl, combine the baking powder and rub. Pat the wings dry with a paper towel, add to the bowl, and toss with the rub mixture to coat. The baking powder will help dry out the exterior of the wings, resulting in extra-crispy skin.

3. Strain the pickle juice into a small pot, add the brown sugar, and heat over medium-high for 1 minute, whisking to make sure the sugar is fully dissolved. Drop the heat to low heat and simmer for 5 minutes. Remove from the heat and let cool. The glaze should be shiny and fairly loose. It will thicken slightly as it cools!

4. Place the chicken wings on the smoker and cook for 30 minutes. Flip and cook for another 30 minutes, or until the internal temperature is at least 165°F (I prefer my wings cooked to about 185ºF because the meat will slide right off the bone).

5. Remove the wings from the grill and immediately brush with the pickle glaze. BE GENTLE, so you do not disrupt the beautiful mahogany color skin you have worked so hard to develop. Serve immediately.

BBQ PEACH-GLAZED CHICKEN KABOBS

SERVES 4 TO 6

Peaches are a summertime staple in my house—our fridge is always stocked with the flavor in the form of jelly or preserves. When they're combined with my classic BBQ sauce, Aidric and Nash devour these chicken kabobs before I can even get them off the grill, and I can even sneak in a few vegetables!

1 tablespoon peach preserves

¼ cup Classic Sweet BBQ Sauce (page 147)

1 tablespoon honey

1 tablespoon apple cider vinegar

1 teaspoon smoked paprika

½ teaspoon garlic powder

Kosher salt and freshly cracked black pepper

1½ pounds boneless, skinless chicken breast, cut into cubes

24 ounce package of button mushrooms

1 green bell pepper

1 red bell pepper

1 yellow bell pepper

2 red onions, quartered

10 ounces cherry tomatoes

Special equipment: metal or wooden skewers

1. If using wooden skewers, soak them in water to cover for at least 30 minutes to prevent burning.

2. Preheat your grill to medium-high heat.

3. Whisk the peach preserves, BBQ sauce, honey, vinegar, smoked paprika, and garlic powder in a large bowl. Season with salt and pepper.

4. Add the chicken cubes to the peach glaze, mixing to ensure each piece is coated evenly. Cover and refrigerate for at least 30 minutes.

5. Skewer the marinated chicken cubes, alternating with the mushrooms, bell peppers, onions, and cherry tomatoes.

6. Set the kabobs on the preheated grill and cook, rotating every 3 to 4 minutes and brushing the remaining peach glaze on the kabobs, for a total of 15 to 20 minutes.

7. Serve the kabobs immediately.

JERK MARINATED CHICKEN THIGHS

SERVES 4 TO 6

When it comes to vacation spots, Jamaica is one of my all-time favorite destinations. Kristin and I have visited four times (and counting), and we are always blown away by the country's natural beauty, rich culture, and delicious food. My favorite flavor on our trips is always jerk seasoning. One of my colleagues at school was born in Jamaica, and whenever he visits, he's kind enough to bring his pop's famous jerk seasoning so I can get my fix without traveling to the Caribbean. I've begged and begged him for the recipe, but to no avail—so until I can convince him, here's my best shot at replicating this irresistible tangy, savory, and sweet Jamaican staple.

For the Jerk Seasoning:

1 tablespoon garlic powder

1 tablespoon onion powder

1 tablespoon brown sugar

2 to 3 teaspoons cayenne pepper

2 teaspoons kosher salt

2 teaspoons freshly cracked black pepper

2 teaspoons ground ginger

2 teaspoons dried thyme

2 teaspoons dried parsley

2 teaspoons smoked paprika

½ teaspoon ground cinnamon

½ teaspoon ground allspice

½ teaspoon ground nutmeg

1. Make the jerk seasoning: In a small bowl, mix the garlic powder, onion powder, brown sugar, cayenne, salt, pepper, ginger, thyme, parsley, smoked paprika, cinnamon, allspice, and nutmeg. This recipe makes ½ cup and can be stored in a sealed container for up to 2 years.

2. Make the wet rub: Combine ¼ cup of the jerk seasoning with the oil, lime juice, and soy sauce. In a large bowl, rub the chicken thighs with the wet rub until well coated (be sure to season under the skin). Cover the bowl with plastic wrap and refrigerate for at least 2 hours or overnight.

3. Preheat your grill to medium-high heat.

4. Place the marinated chicken thighs on the grill skin-side up. Grill over direct heat for 5 to 6 minutes. Flip to skin-side down and grill for another 4 minutes. Repeat this process moving between areas of the grill. This will help to prevent flare-ups from the fat. Grill for 20 to 25 minutes total, until you reach an internal temperature of 185°F.

CHEAT SHEET

- Bone-in, skin-on chicken thighs are ideal for jerk chicken, as they remain juicy and flavorful during cooking. The bone helps to retain moisture, while the skin adds flavor and protects the meat.

- For maximum flavor, marinate the chicken thighs in the jerk marinade overnight in the refrigerator. This allows the spices and seasonings to penetrate the meat for a more flavorful chicken.

For the Wet Rub:

¼ cup jerk seasoning

¼ cup extra virgin olive oil

Juice of 1 lime

2 tablespoons reduced-sodium soy sauce

For the Chicken:

6 to 8 bone-in, skin-on chicken thighs

1 lime

While the FDA recommendation for chicken is 165ºF, thighs may still be tough and stringy at that temperature. When cooked to between 175°F and 185°F, the connective tissue will melt and result in a juicy and tender piece of chicken!

5. Squeeze the lime over the chicken and serve as soon as possible.

HONEY-MUSTARD GLAZED WINGS

SERVES 4 TO 6

Like most kids, Aidric and Nash love finger foods. Getting them to use utensils is like trying to get my vegetarian wife to try some of my meat recipes! Fortunately, one of their favorite foods is chicken wings, so I created this recipe using their favorite condiment: honey mustard. Sweet, tangy, sticky, and incredibly messy, these have been a hit from the first time I made them.

2 to 3 pounds chicken wings

Kosher salt and freshly cracked black pepper

¼ cup Dijon mustard

¼ cup honey

2 tablespoons apple cider vinegar

2 tablespoons soy sauce

2 cloves garlic, minced

1 tablespoon chopped fresh parsley (optional)

1. Preheat your grill to medium-high heat.

2. Season the chicken wings with salt and pepper.

3. Whisk the mustard, honey, vinegar, soy sauce, and garlic in a small saucepan. Cook over medium heat, frequently stirring, until the mixture thickens, about 5 minutes.

4. Place the chicken wings on the preheated grill. Grill, flipping the wings and moving them around the grill every 3 to 4 minutes. Moving them will help prevent flare-ups from fat from the skin. Brush the honey-mustard glaze onto the wings every 5 to 7 minutes. You will begin to see a deep golden brown caramelization of the glaze, which is exactly what we want.

5. Continue cooking and flipping until the wings reach an internal temperature of 185°F for a delicious and tender fall-off-the-bone wing!

6. Remove the wings from the grill and sprinkle with the parsley (if using). Serve immediately.

CHEAT SHEET

Double the recipe for the sauce so you have some extra to serve on the side. Ranch dressing, blue cheese dressing, and barbecue sauce are also great options.

SMOKED BBQ BACON-WRAPPED DRUMSTICKS

SERVES 4 TO 6

In my opinion, drumsticks are the best part of a chicken. However, when you're using a smoker, it can be difficult to get the skin super crispy. Of course, you can always grill the drumsticks over direct heat after smoking to get that satisfying crunch—or you can use bacon. Guess which option I prefer? Yes, let's remove that potentially rubbery skin from the drumsticks and replace it with bacon. The result is an incredibly juicy piece of chicken wrapped in a blanket of perfectly smoked and rendered bacon!

12 chicken drumsticks

2 tablespoons mustard

All-Purpose BBQ Rub
(page 150)

1 pound regular-cut bacon
(typically 16 strips)

¼ cup Classic Sweet BBQ Sauce
(page 147), plus more for
serving

1. Preheat your smoker to 250°F.

2. Remove the skin from the drumsticks, starting at the thick part of the drumstick and pulling down to the thin part of the leg. Use a paper towel to get a nice grip of the slippery skin and it will pull right off.

3. Place the drumsticks in a gallon zip-top bag and coat the chicken with the mustard. The mustard is going to act as a binder for the BBQ rub and the zip-top bag is NO MESS! Add the rub and massage the bag with your hands until the chicken is completely coated with seasoning.

4. Wrap a strip of bacon around each drumstick, securing it with toothpicks if needed. Feel free to add a little more rub to the bacon.

5. Place the drumsticks on the smoker and cook for 1 hour, or until the internal temperature of the chicken is 165°F to 170°F. You'll know it's ready when the bacon is that beautiful mahogany color we all know and love.

6. While still on the smoker, brush the drumsticks with the BBQ sauce and continue smoking for another 15 to 20 minutes, until they reach an internal temperature of 175°F to 185°F.

7. Remove the drumsticks from the grill and allow them to rest for 5 minutes. Serve with some extra BBQ sauce on the side.

Period 3
MEAT OF THE SEA

SEAFOOD

There are plenty of reasons to be a little intimidated by seafood on the grill. Lobster, shrimp, and fish are all very delicate and can easily be overcooked. Time and temperature play a huge role in ending up with flaky, chargrilled, flavorful fish or a tough, rubbery piece of shrimp or lobster. I now turn to the grill almost every time I make seafood at the house. I enjoy it so much that in the most pressure-filled moment of my culinary life—on *Next Level Chef*—I made grilled lobster in my elimination round, and it was the dish Gordon Ramsay said I did not deserve to be sent home on!

- Smoky Salmon Bites with Dill Dipping Sauce
- Smoked Garlic Butter Lobster Tails
- Smoked Lemon Herb Whole Branzino
- Cast-Iron Salmon Burgers
- Cast-Iron Shrimp Scampi
- Grilled Lemon Garlic Scallops
- Cedar Plank Salmon
- Grilled Fish Tacos with Chipotle Lime Dressing
- Grilled Garlic-Lime Shrimp Skewers with Vegetables

SMOKED SALMON BITES
WITH **DILL DIPPING SAUCE**

SERVES 6

These small cubed pieces of smoked salmon are best served alongside a creamy dill dipping sauce. The salmon is rich and flavorful with a hint of smokiness, while the dip adds a cool and tangy finish. It's a perfect combination of savory and creamy, making it a delicious appetizer or snack option for any occasion.

For the Salmon:

2 pounds skinless salmon, cut into 1-inch cubes

¼ cup All-Purpose BBQ Rub (150) or another rub

For the Creamy Dill Dipping Sauce:

½ cup mayonnaise

½ cup sour cream

2 tablespoons finely chopped fresh dill (or 1 tablespoon dried dill)

1 tablespoon lemon juice

1 clove garlic, minced

Kosher salt and freshly cracked black pepper

1. Preheat your smoker to 275°F. Add a couple chunks of apple or hickory wood.

2. Season the salmon cubes with the rub, ensuring each piece is coated evenly.

3. Place the seasoned salmon cubes in the smoker and cook for about 30 minutes, until they reach an internal temperature of 145ºF.

4. While the salmon cooks, make the creamy dill dipping sauce. In a medium bowl, mix the mayonnaise and sour cream until smooth and creamy.

5. Add the dill, lemon juice, and garlic, season with salt and pepper, and stir until the ingredients are evenly distributed.

6. Once the salmon cubes have reached an internal temperature of 145°F, remove them from the smoker and let them cool for 5 minutes.

7. Serve the smoked salmon bites with the dipping sauce alongside.

CHEAT SHEET

To add a touch of freshness, sprinkle some chopped fresh dill or parsley over the smoked salmon before serving.

SMOKED GARLIC BUTTER LOBSTER TAILS

My dad always tells me that I was the kid who ordered the most expensive thing on the menu, no matter the restaurant. Eventually, he would give in, and I got to give the pricier item, like lobster, a try. In the years since then, and throughout my BBQ journey, I have had the chance to cook lobster quite often. This recipe combines the luxurious flavor of smoked lobster tails with a luscious garlic butter twist. The delicate smokiness elevates the sweet and succulent lobster meat, while the garlic butter adds richness and depth. Prepare your smoker and get ready to savor every mouthwatering bite.

4 to 6 lobster tails

Kosher salt and freshly cracked black pepper

4 tablespoons (½ stick) unsalted butter

4 cloves garlic, minced

2 tablespoons fresh lemon juice

2 tablespoons chopped fresh parsley

1. Preheat your smoker to 275°F with a couple chunks of applewood. This moderate temperature allows the lobster tails to cook slowly and gently, and the applewood infuses the lobster with smoky flavors while remaining tender and succulent.

2. Use kitchen shears or a sharp knife to carefully cut along the top (or back) of the lobster tail shell. Start near the wide end and cut all the way to the tail. Gently pry the shell open using your hands, making sure to keep the flesh attached at the base of the tail. Lift and pull the meat out from the shell. Gently place the lobster back on top of the shell. Season the lobster tails with salt and pepper.

3. In a small nonstick saucepan, melt the butter over low heat. Add the garlic and cook for 1 to 2 minutes, until fragrant. Stir in the lemon juice and parsley to create a flavorful garlic butter sauce.

4. Place the seasoned lobster tails in the smoker and cook for about 30 minutes, until the internal temperature reaches 135°F.

5. Take the lobster tails out of the smoker and brush the garlic butter generously over the meat.

6. Serve immediately and savor the luscious combination of smoky lobster with that aromatic garlic butter sauce.

CHEAT SHEET

- Consider adding a sprinkle of smoked paprika or a dash of cayenne pepper to the garlic butter mixture for an extra hint of smokiness or a touch of heat.

- For an impressive presentation, garnish the smoked lobster tails with additional chopped parsley and a squeeze of lemon juice.

SMOKED LEMON HERB WHOLE BRANZINO

SERVES 2

My time on *Next Level Chef* was cut short by a thirty-pound whole halibut I had to break down into fillets for myself and my teammates. Let's just say I'll stick to butchering brisket! My solution for fish is to go smaller and grill it whole. This whole grilled branzino infused with aromatic herbs and a burst of citrus perfectly absorbs the smoky essence and chargrilled flavor, creating an absolute burst of flavors.

2 whole branzinos, gutted and scaled

Kosher salt and freshly cracked black pepper

1. Preheat your grill to medium-high heat. Make sure the grill grates are clean and well-oiled to prevent sticking.

2. Sprinkle or brush the insides of the branzinos with salt and pepper.

1 lemon, sliced into rounds

4 sprigs fresh rosemary

4 sprigs fresh thyme

2 cloves garlic, minced

4 tablespoons extra virgin olive oil

3. Stuff the cavities of the branzinos with lemon rounds, rosemary, thyme, and garlic. These aromatic herbs and citrus slices will infuse the fish with some amazing flavors.

4. Brush the branzinos with the oil to keep them moist and prevent sticking to the grill grates.

5. Place the prepared branzinos directly on the grill grates and close the lid. Grill for 6 to 8 minutes per side, until the flesh is fully cooked and flakes easily with a fork. The exact cooking time will depend on the size of the fish and the heat of your grill.

6. Carefully flip the branzinos using a spatula or grilling tongs to ensure the delicate skin stays intact.

7. Once the branzinos are cooked through and have beautiful grill marks on both sides, remove them from the grill and let rest for a few minutes. The internal temperature of the fully cooked fish should be 145°F and you will notice the flesh turn from translucent to opaque.

8. Serve immediately and enjoy this tender and flavorful fish!

CHEAT SHEET

- Adjust the grilling time based on the thickness of the branzino and the heat of your grill. It's better to slightly undercook the fish and let it rest, as the residual heat will continue cooking it.

- For an extra burst of citrusy flavor, squeeze some fresh lemon juice over the smoked branzino just before serving.

CAST-IRON SALMON BURGERS

SERVES 4

Whether you're a seafood enthusiast or a burger connoisseur, this cast-iron salmon burger is the best of both worlds. The sizzle of the grill meets the savoriness of a cast-iron skillet to create a burger with a crispy char, balanced flavors, and perfectly flaky salmon in every bite.

1 pound fresh salmon fillets, skin removed

¼ cup breadcrumbs

¼ cup finely chopped red onion

2 cloves garlic, minced

2 tablespoons capers, chopped

2 tablespoons chopped fresh dill

Zest and juice of 1 lemon

1 egg

Kosher salt and freshly cracked black pepper

Oil, for brushing the pan

4 hamburger buns

Lettuce, tomato slices, and other favorite burger toppings

1. Preheat your grill to medium-high heat, setting up a two-zone cooking area with direct and indirect heat. Place a large cast-iron skillet on the grill grates to preheat.

2. Cut the salmon fillets into small pieces and place them in a food processor. Pulse until the salmon is finely chopped but not pureed.

3. In a large bowl, combine the chopped salmon, breadcrumbs, red onion, garlic, capers, dill, lemon zest, lemon juice, and egg and season with salt and pepper. Gently mix until the ingredients are well combined.

4. Divide the salmon mixture into 4 equal portions and shape them into burger patties that are compacted but not too tightly packed.

5. Brush the preheated cast-iron skillet with oil and place the salmon burgers on it. Grill for 4 to 5 minutes on each side, until the burgers are cooked through and have some nice brow and the internal temperature reaches 145°F.

6. During the last minute of grilling, place the burger buns on the grill, cut-side down, to toast lightly.

7. To assemble, place a lettuce leaf on the bottom bun, followed by a grilled salmon patty. Top with tomato slices, red onion, and any other burger toppings you like. Finish with the top bun.

CHEAT SHEET

- Start with fresh, high-quality salmon fillets with firm flesh and a bright, vibrant color.

- Be careful not to overprocess the salmon, as you want to maintain some texture for the burgers.

CAST-IRON SHRIMP SCAMPI

SERVES 4

Until I discovered this recipe, almost all my experience with cast iron had been for getting an incredible sear on a beautiful steak. Let's break out the cast-iron skillet, throw it on the grill, and get it sizzling with this simple, can't-miss shrimp scampi. The succulent shrimp, garlic, and white wine create a combination worthy of any menu.

1 pound large shrimp, peeled and deveined

2 tablespoons RubCily La Chingadera Rub and Taco Seasoning (or 1 tablespoon kosher salt and 1 tablespoon freshly cracked black pepper)

4 tablespoons (½ stick) unsalted butter

4 cloves garlic, minced

¼ cup white wine

Juice of 1 lemon

2 tablespoons chopped fresh parsley

Red pepper flakes (optional)

Crusty bread, for serving

1. Preheat your grill to medium heat. Place a large cast-iron skillet on the grill grates to preheat.

2. Put the shrimp in a large bowl and season with the rub.

3. Melt the butter in the preheated skillet. Add the garlic and cook, stirring, until fragrant, about 1 minute.

4. Stir in the wine and lemon juice and simmer for a minute or two.

5. Add the shrimp to the skillet and cook for 3 to 4 minutes on each side, until they turn pink and are fully cooked.

6. Remove the shrimp from the heat and sprinkle with the parsley and red pepper flakes (if using).

7. Serve with crusty bread on the side to soak up the delicious garlic butter sauce.

CHEAT SHEET

- For added flavor and kick, sprinkle a pinch of red pepper flakes into the skillet along with the garlic.

- Be careful not to overcook the shrimp, as they can become tough and rubbery. They should turn pink and curl into a "C" shape when cooked.

- Serve the shrimp scampi over pasta or alongside a fresh green salad for a complete meal.

GRILLED LEMON GARLIC SCALLOPS

SERVES 4

When it comes to tailgating at Philadelphia Eagles games, scallops are always on the menu. Which means that over the years, I have cooked scallops more than any other seafood. These grilled scallops infused with zesty lemon and garlicky goodness are a fan favorite. The slight char from the grill adds a touch of smokiness that pairs perfectly with a burst of freshness from the lemon and the aromatic garlic.

1 pound large scallops

Kosher salt and freshly cracked black pepper

2 tablespoons extra virgin olive oil

2 cloves garlic, minced

Juice of 2 lemons, plus lemon wedges for serving

2 tablespoons chopped fresh parsley, plus more for garnish

1. Preheat your grill to high heat.

2. Place the scallops on a plate, season with salt and pepper, and pat them dry with paper towels.

3. In a small bowl, whisk the oil, garlic, lemon juice, and parsley to create a marinade.

4. Brush the scallops with the lemon-garlic marinade, making sure they are evenly coated.

5. Place the scallops on the grill and cook for 2 to 3 minutes on each side, until they develop a beautiful char and are cooked through. Avoid overcrowding the scallops on the grill so they cook evenly.

6. Remove the grilled scallops from the heat to a plate and let them rest for a couple of minutes.

7. Garnish with parsley and enjoy these succulent and flavorful scallops with lemon wedges for squeezing!

CHEAT SHEET

Make sure the grill grates are well oiled to prevent the scallops from sticking.

CEDAR PLANK SALMON

Thanks to the rustic flavors of a cedar plank, this recipe is one of the tastiest and simplest salmon dishes you can make. The marinade of lemon, garlic, dill, and honey creates remarkable flavor, and the contrast of the crust and the smoky tenderness of the fish will blow you away! So set the salmon on the cedar plank and let all that smokiness envelop the fish!

4 salmon fillets, skin removed

Kosher salt and freshly cracked black pepper

¼ cup extra virgin olive oil

Juice of 2 lemons, plus lemon wedges for serving

4 cloves garlic, minced

2 tablespoons chopped fresh dill, plus more for garnish

1 tablespoon honey

Special equipment: 4 cedar planks, soaked in water for at least 1 hour

1. Preheat your grill to medium-high heat.

2. Season the salmon fillets with salt and pepper.

3. In a small bowl, whisk the oil, lemon juice, garlic, dill, and honey to create a marinade.

4. Brush the salmon fillets with the marinade, making sure they are well coated.

5. Place the soaked cedar planks on the preheated grill and let them heat up for a few minutes.

6. Place the salmon fillets on the cedar planks flesh-side up.

7. Cover and cook for 15 to 20 minutes, until the flesh is opaque and flakes easily with a fork.

8. Remove the salmon from the grill and let rest for a few minutes.

9. Serve garnished with dill and with lemon wedges alongside.

CHEAT SHEET

- Soaking the cedar planks in water for at least 1 hour helps prevent them from burning during grilling.

- If you prefer a more pronounced smoky flavor, lightly toast the cedar planks on the grill before placing the salmon on top.

- Feel free to experiment with different herbs, such as rosemary or thyme, for variety.

GRILLED FISH TACOS WITH CHIPOTLE LIME DRESSING

SERVES 4

If fish tacos are on the menu, sign me up! This recipe is a fiesta of flavors, between the smoky grilled fish, tender tortillas, and zesty chipotle lime dressing, which offers a delightfully cool kick. Charred grill marks complement the creamy and tangy dressing perfectly. This is a great meal to make for a refreshing lunch, a crowd-pleasing dinner, and, of course, Taco Tuesday.

For the Tacos:

1 pound white fish fillets (such as halibut or tilapia)

Kosher salt and freshly cracked black pepper

1 tablespoon extra virgin olive oil

8 small flour tortillas

½ head green cabbage, cut in half, cored, and shredded

2 avocados, diced

½ red onion, diced

1 cup fresh cilantro leaves

Lime wedges, for serving

For the Chipotle Lime Dressing:

½ cup mayonnaise

1 chipotle pepper in adobo sauce, chopped

Juice of 2 limes

1 clove garlic, minced

Kosher salt and freshly cracked black pepper to taste

1. Preheat your grill to medium-high heat.

2. Season the fish fillets with salt and pepper, then drizzle with the oil.

3. Place the fish fillets on the preheated grill and cook for 5 to 7 minutes on each side, until the fish is opaque and flakes easily with a fork.

4. While the fish is grilling, prepare the chipotle lime dressing. Combine the mayonnaise, chipotle, lime juice, garlic, salt, and pepper in a bowl. Mix well until smooth and creamy.

5. Remove the grilled fish from the heat and let it rest for a few minutes.

6. Warm the flour tortillas on the grill for a few seconds on each side.

7. To assemble the tacos, place a few pieces of grilled fish onto each warm tortilla. Top with cabbage, avocado, red onion, cilantro leaves, and a drizzle of chipotle lime dressing.

8. Serve the tacos immediately with lime wedges on the side.

CHEAT SHEET

- You can use a grilling basket or aluminum foil to prevent the fish from sticking to the grill grates.

- Adjust the spice level of the chipotle lime dressing by adding more or less chipotle pepper according to your preference.

- For a smoky touch, lightly grill the tortillas until they have a slight char.

CHEAT SHEET

- Be careful not to overcook the shrimp, as they can become rubbery. Keep a close eye on them and remove them from the grill as soon as they turn pink and opaque.

GRILLED GARLIC-LIME SHRIMP SKEWERS WITH VEGETABLES

SERVES 4

These skewers quickly became a summer barbecue staple at my house. The shrimp is marinated in zesty garlic and lime, and the colorful vegetables make this dish even more vibrant and delicious. They're great to serve as an appetizer, as a main course with a side salad, or even as a filling for tacos and wraps. Plus, these skewers are quick, easy to make, and can even be made vegetarian—just eliminate the shrimp and pile on the veggies!

3 cloves garlic, minced

Zest and juice of 1 lime, plus more lime juice to finish

2 tablespoons extra virgin olive oil

1 tablespoon chopped fresh cilantro, plus more for garnish

½ teaspoon salt

¼ teaspoon freshly ground black pepper

1 pound large shrimp, peeled and deveined

Assorted vegetables (bell peppers, onions, cherry tomatoes), cut into bite-sized pieces

Special equipment: wooden or metal skewers

1. Preheat your grill to medium-high heat.

2. If using wooden skewers, soak them in water for at least 30 minutes to prevent burning.

3. In a large bowl, combine the garlic, lime zest, lime juice, oil, cilantro, salt, and black pepper. Mix well.

4. Add the shrimp to the bowl and toss them in the marinade until they are well coated. Let them marinate on the counter for 15 to 20 minutes.

5. Thread the shrimp and vegetables onto the skewers, alternating between shrimp and vegetables.

6. Place the skewers on the preheated grill and cook for 2 to 3 minutes per side, until the shrimp turn pink and opaque and the vegetables are slightly charred and tender.

7. Remove the skewers from the grill and let them rest for a few minutes.

8. Garnish the skewers with cilantro, squeeze some additional lime juice (if using) over the skewers, and serve.

Period 4
WILD GAME

LAMB, VEAL, AND ELK

What is the one dish that you are ordering when it's on the menu every single time without hesitation? For me, it is almost any lamb dish, but specifically a rack of lamb! Five to seven years ago, I stepped outside of my safe, convenient, little box filled with beef and chicken and dove headfirst into the world of lamb, veal, and even some game meat, like elk (which is AMAZING!). So fire up the coals and consider the following recipes the encouragement you need to step out of that comfort zone.

- Smoked Leg of Lamb with Garlic and Rosemary
- Smoked and Grilled Rack of Lamb
- Grilled Lamb Loin Chops
- Lamb Kabobs with Tzatziki
- Goat Cheese–Stuffed Veal Burgers
- Next-Level Bone-In Veal Chop with Bacon and Bell Pepper Ragu
- Elk Burgers with Caramelized Onions and Blue Cheese
- Grilled Elk Tenderloin with Herb Butter

SMOKED LEG OF LAMB WITH GARLIC AND ROSEMARY

SERVES 10 TO 12

A whole leg of lamb is not something you will typically prepare on a passing Tuesday, but it is perfect for special occasions or gatherings. When I'm cooking lamb, I like to stay pretty traditional with the aromatic flavors of garlic and rosemary and just the right hint of smoke. There are very few things that will impress your company like a tableside carving—and a leg of lamb will do exactly that.

One 3- to 5-pound leg of lamb

5 cloves garlic, minced

2 tablespoons chopped fresh rosemary

Kosher salt and freshly cracked black pepper to taste

3 tablespoons extra virgin olive oil

1. Prepare the lamb by trimming excess fat and removing the silver skin. Mix the garlic, rosemary, salt, pepper, and oil in a small bowl to form a paste.

2. Rub the paste all over the lamb, making sure to get it into every crevice. Allow the lamb to sit at room temperature for at least 30 minutes or up to 2 hours. For added flavor, consider marinating overnight in the refrigerator before smoking.

3. Preheat your smoker to 275°F.

4. Place the lamb on the smoker, making sure to keep it away from direct heat. Cook the lamb until the internal temperature reaches 145°F.

5. Experiment with different types of wood, such as hickory or applewood, for unique flavor profiles.

6. Let the smoked leg of lamb rest for 15 minutes before carving. This allows the juices to redistribute and ensures a moist and flavorful lamb.

SMOKED AND GRILLED RACK OF LAMB

SERVES 4

When I was sixteen, I worked in a banquet hall, and one of the staple dishes was leg of lamb accompanied by a little stainless steel ramekin of mint jelly. So now, when I think of rack of lamb, I instantly think of mint jelly! For this recipe, I wanted to take that nostalgia of my youth to the next level by finishing with a traditional twist of mint chimichurri. With a tender and smoky exterior and aromatic garlic and rosemary, this dish is perfect for impressing guests at special occasions and gatherings and hopefully will spark some nostalgia, too.

For the Lamb:

2 racks of lamb, frenched

Kosher salt and freshly cracked black pepper

2 tablespoons extra virgin olive oil

3 cloves garlic, minced

2 tablespoons chopped fresh rosemary

Zest and juice of 1 lemon

For the Mint Chimichurri:

2 cloves garlic, chopped

1 cup packed fresh mint leaves

1 cup packed fresh Italian parsley leaves

2 tablespoons red wine vinegar

½ teaspoon kosher salt

¼ teaspoon red pepper flakes

6 tablespoons extra virgin olive oil

1. Preheat your smoker to 275°F. I like a sweet and subtle smokiness for lamb, so I use a fruitwood like apple, cherry, or peach.

2. Season the racks of lamb with salt and pepper.

3. In a small bowl, combine oil, garlic, rosemary, lemon zest, and lemon juice.

4. Rub the mixture all over the racks of lamb, ensuring they are evenly coated.

5. Place the lamb in the smoker or grill, using indirect heat, and cook for 45 minutes to 1 hour, to an internal temperature of 120°F.

6. Increase the heat on your grill.

7. Move the racks of lamb to direct heat and cook for 2 to 3 minutes on each side to achieve a beautifully browned exterior.

8. Remove the lamb from the grill when it reaches an internal temperature of 130°F, and let it rest for 5 to 10 minutes on a cutting board before slicing.

CHEAT SHEET

- Trim excess fat from the rack, leaving a thin layer to add flavor and moisture during cooking. Too much fat can make the lamb greasy, so it's important to trim it well.

- Use a sharp knife to slice the rack of lamb into individual chops. For an elegant presentation, slice between the bones to create evenly sized chops.

GRILLED LAMB LOIN CHOPS

SERVES 4

Grilled lamb loin chops are a go-to part of the rotation in my house, especially when the boys and I are looking for a little variety. We go with a salt-and-pepper-based rub like my RubCity Texas Hat Hanger BBQ Rub and Seasoning, but you can use another all-purpose seasoning. I grill these using the indirect (two-zone) method, which simply means you will have a cool zone and a hot zone. Starting on the cool zone to cook them slowly will help maintain the juiciness, and finishing them over the flame for those beautiful grill marks that will lock in that flavor.

4 lamb loin chops, 1 inch thick

2 tablespoons extra virgin olive oil

2 tablespoons RubCity Texas Hat Hanger BBQ Rub and Seasoning or another rub

1. Preheat your grill to 425°F, then turn off half of the burners for indirect two-zone cooking. For a charcoal grill, simply push your coals to one side.

2. Put the lamb chops in a bowl, drizzle the oil over them, and then sprinkle the rub evenly over them.

3. Use your hands to pat the rub into the lamb chops, making sure they are well coated on all sides.

4. Place the lamb chops on the cool side of the grill, close the lid, and cook to an internal temperature of 110°F, 8 to 10 minutes. Move them over to the direct heat side and grill for 2 minutes on each side, until they are cooked to your liking. I prefer 135°F for a nice light pink center.

5. Remove the lamb chops from the grill and let them rest for at least 5 minutes before serving.

CHEAT SHEET

If using a charcoal grill, add soaked wood chips directly to the coals for a smoky flavor.

LAMB KABOBS WITH TZATZIKI

SERVES 8

In 2004, I had the amazing opportunity to spend two weeks in Athens, Greece, for the Summer Olympics. It was an experience of a lifetime, and when I think back, lamb and tzatziki are the flavors I taste. These kabobs, marinated with garlic, herbs, and a touch of lemon to keep them bright and zesty and finished with tangy, cool tzatziki, are a delicious and easy way to enjoy tender lamb. And the flavors from this recipe just may get stuck in your memory as well.

For the Kabobs:

One 2-pound boneless leg of lamb, cut into 1-inch cubes

2 red bell peppers, cut into pieces

2 yellow bell peppers, cut into pieces

1 red onion, cut into 1-inch pieces

1 pint cherry tomatoes

4 cloves garlic, minced

½ cup extra virgin olive oil

Juice of 1 lemon

2 teaspoons ground cumin

2 teaspoons onion powder

1 teaspoon smoked paprika

1 tablespoon kosher salt

2 teaspoons freshly cracked black pepper

Special equipment: 8 wooden or metal skewers

1. If using wooden skewers, soak them in water for at least 30 minutes to prevent burning.

2. Thread the lamb onto the skewers, alternating with the peppers, onions, and tomatoes, repeating until all 8 skewers are made. Place the skewers in a pan with a high edge in a single layer and set aside.

3. In a small bowl, whisk the garlic, oil, lemon juice, cumin, onion powder, paprika, salt, pepper, parsley, and mint to combine.

4. Pour the mixture over the kabobs, cover with plastic wrap, and refrigerate for 1 hour. Rotate the kabobs halfway through to marinate the other side.

5. Prepare the tzatziki: Peel the cucumber, then grate it using a box grater. You can also use a food processor with a grating attachment. Place the cucumber in a fine-mesh strainer or a clean kitchen towel. If using a strainer, sprinkle a little salt over the grated cucumber and let it sit for 15 to 20 minutes to draw out excess moisture. If using a towel, squeeze the cucumber to extract as much liquid as possible.

6. In a medium bowl, mix the yogurt, garlic, oil, lemon juice, and dill until well combined.

7. After draining the cucumber, press it again to remove any remaining moisture, then add the grated cucumber to the yogurt mixture.

For the Tzatziki:

1 cucumber, grated

2 cups full-fat or low-fat plain Greek yogurt

2 or 3 cloves garlic, minced

2 tablespoons extra virgin olive oil

1 tablespoon fresh lemon juice

1 tablespoon finely chopped fresh dill (or 1 teaspoon dried dill)

Kosher salt and freshly ground black pepper

8. Season the tzatziki sauce with salt and pepper. The cucumber will add some natural saltiness, so start with a small amount of salt and adjust as needed. Stir all the ingredients together until well combined.

9. Cover the bowl with plastic wrap or a lid and refrigerate the tzatziki sauce for at least 30 minutes before serving so the flavors can meld and develop.

10. Preheat your grill to medium-high heat.

11. Place the skewers on the preheated grill and cook for 3 to 4 minutes on each side, until the lamb's internal temperature reaches 135°F.

12. Remove the kabobs from the grill and allow them to rest for 5 minutes before serving.

13. Serve the kabobs with the tzatziki.

GOAT CHEESE-STUFFED VEAL BURGERS

SERVES 4

These veal burgers are a delicious twist on the classic beef burger, featuring juicy veal patties filled with luscious goat cheese. Like so many of the recipes in this book, my first time serving these burgers is a memory I hold very close to my heart. My father-in-law would swing by often to just come visit, hang out, and try my latest BBQ creations. I had been wanting to make this recipe for some time, and had recently shopped for the ingredients, so one night when he came over, I figured what better time than NOW! Kristin, being vegetarian, wouldn't be able to provide feedback, so her dad was the perfect person. When I tell you he talked about this burger every time I saw him after that night, I am not exaggerating. He said it was THE BEST burger he has ever eaten—I hope you agree! R.I.P. Pop-Pop Nash ♥

2 pounds ground veal

Kosher salt and freshly cracked black pepper to taste

1 clove garlic, minced

1 tablespoon chopped fresh parsley

½ teaspoon dried basil

4 ounces goat cheese, softened

4 hamburger buns

Toppings of your choice (such as lettuce, tomato, onion)

1. Preheat your grill to medium-high heat.

2. Put the ground veal, salt, pepper, garlic, parsley, and basil in a large bowl. Mix well to combine.

3. Divide the mixture into 8 equal parts and shape each into a patty.

4. Place a portion of the goat cheese in the center of 4 patties and cover each with another patty. Pinch the edges of the patties together to seal the cheese. Make sure the cheese is completely sealed inside to prevent it from oozing out during grilling.

5. Place the burgers on the preheated grill and cook for 5 to 6 minutes on each side, until the internal temperature of the veal reaches 145°F.

6. Toast the hamburger buns on the grill for 1 to 2 minutes.

7. Place a burger on the bottom half of each bun, dress with your desired toppings, and finish with the top half of the bun.

CHEAT SHEET

- Experiment with different toppings, such as caramelized onions, arugula, or roasted red pepper, to customize your burger.

- Serve the burgers with a side of fries or a crisp salad for a complete meal.

NEXT-LEVEL BONE-IN VEAL CHOP WITH BACON AND BELL PEPPER RAGU

SERVES 1

This is a recipe born of sheer panic. On the very first episode of *Next Level Chef*, we were told to make our best next-level dish. By complete luck of the draw, my team began in the "top kitchen," which meant a state-of-the-art kitchen and the best ingredients money could buy at our disposal! I ran to the ingredients platform, and the first thing I saw was a big, thick bone-in veal chop. Decision made. Everything else I grabbed was a blur, but it turned out to be one of the best plates of food I have ever presented. Nyesha Arrington called it "delicious," Gordon Ramsay referred to it as "very chefy," and my mentor, Richard Blais, praised it as being a very cohesive dish, "ready for a restaurant menu." Re-creating this recipe at home will be a little less stressful but just as delicious.

One 2-inch-thick bone-in veal chop

Kosher salt and freshly cracked black pepper

2 slices bacon, diced

1 tablespoon extra virgin olive oil

1 tablespoon unsalted butter

¼ cup diced red bell pepper

¼ cup diced yellow bell pepper

¼ cup diced green bell pepper

1 cup balsamic vinegar

1. Preheat your grill to medium-high heat.

2. While the grill preheats, take the veal chop out of the refrigerator and let it sit at room temperature for about 30 minutes. This will allow for more even cooking.

3. Season the veal chop generously with salt and pepper on both sides.

4. In a medium skillet, cook the bacon over medium heat until it becomes crispy. Remove the bacon from the skillet and place it on a paper towel–lined plate to drain excess grease.

5. Add the oil and butter to the same skillet. Once the butter is melted, add the bell peppers and cook until they are tender, 4 to 5 minutes.

CHEAT SHEET

- Feel free to adjust the seasoning of the ragu, adding herbs like thyme or rosemary for extra flavor if desired.

- Serve the veal chop with roasted potatoes, steamed vegetables, or a refreshing green salad to complement the flavors of the dish.

6. Return the crispy bacon to the pan with the bell peppers and keep warm over low heat.

7. Meanwhile, place the seasoned veal chop on the preheated grill.

8. Grill the veal chop for 6 to 7 minutes on each side, rotating it to create those beautiful grill marks. The internal temperature should reach 140°F for a perfect medium doneness. Keep in mind that the temperature will rise a few degrees as the meat rests.

9. Remove the veal chop from the grill and let it rest for 5 to 10 minutes before serving. This resting time allows the juices to redistribute, resulting in a juicier and more flavorful chop.

10. While the veal is resting, make the balsamic reduction. Pour the vinegar into a small saucepan. Place the saucepan over medium-high heat and bring the vinegar to a gentle boil. Reduce the heat to medium-low and let the vinegar simmer, stirring occasionally to prevent burning, for 10 to 15 minutes, until it has thickened and reduced to about half of its original volume. To test the consistency, dip a spoon into the reduction. It should coat the back of the spoon.

11. Once the vinegar has reached the desired thickness, remove the saucepan from the heat and let it cool down for a few minutes. It will continue to thicken as it cools.

12. Spoon the bacon and bell pepper ragu over the grilled veal chop. Serve with a generous drizzle of your balsamic reduction.

ELK BURGERS WITH CARAMELIZED ONIONS AND BLUE CHEESE

SERVES 4

While beef may be the holy grail of BBQ, elk is quickly becoming a star of its own under my roof. Aidric and Nash have even gone as far to request it over a traditional burger. While elk is extremely lean, it is a very flavorful alternative and is incredibly high in protein. I like to address the leanness with some raw chopped bacon, as it cooks up perfectly with the elk. I find elk to be a bit sweeter than beef and, contrary to what some may think, it is not gamey at all. Caramelized onions and some crumbly blue cheese top it off!

For the Burgers:

1 pound ground elk meat

2 slices bacon, finely chopped

½ teaspoon salt

¼ teaspoon freshly ground black pepper

1½ teaspoons Worcestershire sauce

½ teaspoon garlic powder

½ teaspoon onion powder

8 ounces blue cheese

4 hamburger buns

For the Caramelized Onions:

2 tablespoons butter

1 tablespoon extra virgin olive oil

2 large onions, thinly sliced

1 teaspoon sugar

Kosher salt and freshly cracked black pepper

1. Preheat your grill to medium-high heat.

2. In a large bowl, combine the ground elk meat and chopped bacon with salt and pepper, Worcestershire sauce, garlic powder, and onion powder. Mix well to incorporate evenly.

3. Divide the seasoned elk meat into 4 equal portions and shape each portion into a patty.

4. In a large skillet, melt the butter in the oil over medium heat. Add the onions and cook until they become soft and translucent.

5. Sprinkle the sugar over the onions and continue to cook, stirring occasionally, on medium heat, until the onions are caramelized and golden brown, about 15 to 20 minutes. Season with salt and pepper.

6. Place the elk burgers on the preheated grill and cook for 4 to 5 minutes per side, until they reach your desired level of doneness—I prefer 140°F for a perfect medium.

7. During the last minute of grilling, top each elk burger with 2 ounces of the blue cheese and allow it to melt slightly.

8. Toast the hamburger buns on the grill for a minute or two.

9. Place a patty on the bottom half of each bun, top it with caramelized onions, and finish with the top half of the bun.

CHEAT SHEET

- Elk meat is lean, so avoid overcooking to maintain its juiciness. Cook the burgers to medium-rare or medium doneness.

- You can substitute another type of cheese, such as cheddar or Swiss, for the blue cheese.

- If using a charcoal grill, consider adding soaked wood chips or chunks for a smoky flavor.

GRILLED ELK TENDERLOIN WITH **HERB BUTTER**

SERVES 4

As the name implies, a tenderloin is one of the most tender cuts of meat on any animal. It is a very lean cut of meat, and while its beef counterpart has been known to lack a little in flavor, elk has a slightly sweet taste, is never gamey, and has a perfectly delicate texture. Combined with my very simple herb butter, elk is a new and very versatile option for your grill!

For the Elk:

2 pounds elk tenderloin

Extra virgin olive oil, for brushing

Kosher salt and freshly cracked black pepper

For the Herb Butter:

½ cup (1 stick) unsalted butter, softened

1½ teaspoons chopped fresh rosemary

1½ teaspoons chopped fresh thyme

1½ teaspoons chopped fresh chives

2 cloves garlic, minced

Kosher salt and freshly cracked black pepper

1. Preheat your grill to medium-high heat.

2. Brush the tenderloin with olive oil to prevent sticking to the grill.

3. Season the tenderloin generously with salt and pepper on all sides.

4. Place the tenderloin on the preheated grill and cook, rotating every few minutes to ensure even cooking. After about 15 minutes, the internal temperature should be close to 125°F. Because elk is a very lean meat, I prefer mine cooked to between 130°F to 135°F.

5. While the tenderloin is grilling, prepare the herb butter. In a medium bowl, mix the softened butter, herbs, and garlic and season with salt and pepper. Stir well to combine.

6. Remove the tenderloin from the grill and let it rest on a cutting board for a few minutes to allow the juices to redistribute for optimal tenderness.

7. Slice the tenderloin into medallions and serve them with a dollop of herb butter on top.

CHEAT SHEET

- Because elk tenderloin is a lean and tender cut, be cautious not to overcook it. Aim for medium-rare to medium doneness to preserve its juiciness.

- Experiment with different herbs in the butter to suit your taste preferences. A mixture of dill, chives, and tarragon is one option.

- If using a charcoal grill, consider adding soaked wood chips or chunks for additional smoky flavor.

Period 5
GET SAUCED

SAUCES, RUBS, AND SPICES

What you choose to rub your meat with should never be an afterthought. Barbecue sauce is not just a condiment; it is an integral part of barbecue tradition, enhancing and complementing the smoky, charred flavors of the grill. Whether you prefer sweet, spicy, or tangy, I will guide you through creating and mastering an array of sauces and rubs that will not only complement but elevate your grilling game.

SAUCES

- Alabama White BBQ Sauce
- Mustard-Based BBQ Sauce
- Vinegar-Based Carolina BBQ Sauce
- Classic Sweet BBQ Sauce
- Pickle Glaze

ALABAMA WHITE BBQ SAUCE

Very few sauces can replicate a tangy and creamy Alabama white BBQ sauce. My first experience with this sauce was at Myron Mixon's BBQ Cooking School. The first night we had a meet and greet and a spread that you had to see to believe. Perfectly smoked chicken dripping with Alabama white sauce made with mayonnaise, apple cider vinegar, zesty lemon, and a hint of horseradish—I was hooked! Put a tab in this book and go make some now!

1 cup mayonnaise

½ cup apple cider vinegar

3 tablespoons lemon juice

2 tablespoons jarred horseradish

2 teaspoons sugar

2 teaspoons Dijon mustard

1 teaspoon kosher salt

½ teaspoon freshly ground black pepper

¼ teaspoon cayenne pepper (optional)

1. In a medium bowl, whisk together all the ingredients until well combined.

2. Cover and refrigerate for at least 1 hour before using to allow the flavors to meld.

3. Store in a sealed container in the refrigerator for up to 2 weeks.

MUSTARD-BASED BBQ SAUCE

When I am looking for a burst of bold and tangy flavors with my meat, I turn to this sauce. It's extremely vibrant, with a smooth yellow mustard base and hints of honey and apple cider vinegar. I find its perfect combination of sweet and tangy so versatile for just about anything I pull off the grill, even grilled veggies!

1 cup yellow mustard

¼ cup honey

¼ cup apple cider vinegar

3 tablespoons ketchup

2 tablespoons Worcestershire sauce

2 teaspoons garlic powder

2 teaspoons onion powder

1 teaspoon freshly ground black pepper

1 teaspoon kosher salt

½ teaspoon smoked paprika

¼ teaspoon cayenne pepper (optional)

1. In a medium saucepan, whisk together all the ingredients.

2. Bring to a simmer over medium heat and cook for 5 minutes, whisking occasionally.

3. Remove from the heat and let cool before using.

4. Store in a sealed container in the refrigerator for up to 3 weeks.

VINEGAR-BASED CAROLINA BBQ SAUCE

MAKES ABOUT 1½ CUPS

I have always been a huge fan of vinegar-based sauces. If I am saucing my pulled pork with anything other than its natural juices, this is what I'm reaching for: the perfect amount of spice and tangy sweetness. I always have a couple mason jars in the fridge ready and at my disposal.

1 cup apple cider vinegar

½ cup ketchup

¼ cup brown sugar

2 tablespoons hot sauce, or to taste

2 tablespoons Worcestershire sauce

2 teaspoons garlic powder

2 teaspoons onion powder

1 teaspoon freshly ground black pepper

1 teaspoon kosher salt

½ teaspoon cayenne pepper (optional)

1. In a medium saucepan, whisk together all the ingredients.

2. Bring to a simmer over medium heat and cook for 5 minutes, whisking occasionally.

3. Remove from the heat and let cool before using.

4. Store in a sealed container in the refrigerator for up to 3 weeks.

CLASSIC SWEET BBQ SAUCE

MAKES ABOUT 2 CUPS

Ketchup, molasses, and apple cider vinegar give my classic sweet BBQ sauce its velvety texture, while brown sugar and spices add just the right amount of sweetness and complexity. A versatile option whether you are glazing ribs, basting chicken, or smothering pulled pork.

1½ cups ketchup

½ cup molasses

¼ cup apple cider vinegar

3 tablespoons brown sugar

2 tablespoons Worcestershire sauce

2 teaspoons garlic powder

2 teaspoons onion powder

1 teaspoon freshly ground black pepper

1 teaspoon kosher salt

½ teaspoon smoked paprika

¼ teaspoon cayenne pepper (optional)

1. In a medium saucepan, whisk together all the ingredients.

2. Bring to a simmer over medium heat and cook for 5 minutes, whisking occasionally.

3. Remove from the heat and let cool before using.

4. Store in a sealed container in the refrigerator for up to 3 weeks.

PICKLE GLAZE

MAKES ABOUT 1 CUP

Give your grilled meats an unexpected twist with this pickle glaze. I first learned of this recipe from world-renowned chef Michael Symon and have added some of my favorite flavors to make it my own! Made with the flavorful essence of pickle juice, honey, brown sugar, mustard, and a hint of garlic, this glaze creates a balance of sweet and tangy that will elevate your dishes to a new level of deliciousness. Ideal for brushing over chicken or pork, this pickle glaze will be a crowd-pleasing addition!

½ cup pickle juice

½ cup dark brown sugar

¼ cup honey

2 tablespoons Dijon mustard

1 teaspoon garlic powder

½ teaspoon freshly ground black pepper

¼ teaspoon kosher salt

1. In a small bowl, whisk all the ingredients until well combined.

2. Brush the glaze over grilled meats during the last few minutes of cooking.

3. Store in a sealed container in the refrigerator for up to 3 weeks.

RUBS AND SPICES

Variety is the spice of life! Well, let us embrace that, because I have gathered a handful of my most used rubs and seasonings for you. All-purpose, sweet and spicy, coffee, and poultry, to name a few of my favorites. If it is the regionality and culture of BBQ that you love, you should check out my Memphis-Style Rib Rub (for more than just ribs). With these flavors, you will be armed and ready with everything you need to bring all the flavor to your next cook!

- All-Purpose BBQ Rub
- Sweet and Spicy Pork Rub
- Poultry Rub
- Coffee Dry Rub
- Memphis-Style Rib Rub
- Blackened Cajun Seasoning

ALL-PURPOSE BBQ RUB

½ cup brown sugar

¼ cup paprika

2 tablespoons kosher salt

2 tablespoons freshly ground black pepper

2 tablespoons garlic powder

2 tablespoons onion powder

1 tablespoon chili powder

1 tablespoon cayenne pepper (more or less to desired spiciness)

1. In a medium bowl, mix all the ingredients until well combined.

2. Store in an airtight container in a cool, dry place for up to 6 months.

SWEET AND SPICY PORK RUB

¼ cup brown sugar

2 tablespoons paprika

2 tablespoons chili powder

1 tablespoon ground cumin

1 tablespoon garlic powder

1 tablespoon onion powder

1 tablespoon freshly ground black pepper

1 teaspoon cayenne pepper (more or less to desired spiciness)

½ teaspoon kosher salt

1. In a medium bowl, mix all the ingredients until well combined.

2. Massage the rub all over pork ribs or pork butt before grilling or roasting.

3. Store in an airtight container in a cool, dry place for up to 6 months.

POULTRY RUB

1 tablespoon dried thyme

1 tablespoon dried rosemary

1 tablespoon dried sage

1 tablespoon dried oregano

1 tablespoon dried parsley

1 teaspoon garlic powder

1 teaspoon onion powder

1 teaspoon freshly ground black pepper

½ teaspoon kosher salt

1. In a small bowl, mix all the ingredients until well combined.

2. Massage the rub all over chicken or turkey before grilling or roasting.

3. Store in an airtight container in a cool, dry place for up to 6 months.

COFFEE DRY RUB

½ cup finely ground coffee

½ cup brown sugar

¼ cup paprika

¼ cup chili powder

4 teaspoons garlic powder

4 teaspoons onion powder

4 teaspoons freshly ground black pepper

1 teaspoon kosher salt

1 teaspoon cayenne pepper (optional)

1. In a medium bowl, mix all the ingredients until well combined.

2. Massage the rub onto beef, pork, or game before grilling.

3. Store in an airtight container in a cool, dry place for up to 6 months.

MEMPHIS-STYLE RIB RUB

½ cup paprika

½ cup brown sugar

¼ cup chili powder

¼ cup garlic powder

¼ cup onion powder

2 tablespoons ground mustard

2 tablespoons ground cumin

2 tablespoons freshly ground black pepper

2 teaspoons cayenne pepper (more or less to desired spiciness)

2 teaspoons kosher salt

1. In a medium bowl, mix all the ingredients until well combined.

2. Massage the rub onto ribs or other meats before smoking or grilling.

3. Store in an airtight container in a cool, dry place for up to 6 months.

BLACKENED CAJUN SEASONING

1 tablespoon paprika

2 tablespoons smoked paprika

1 teaspoon dried thyme

1 teaspoon dried oregano

1 teaspoon garlic powder

1 tablespoon onion powder

1 teaspoon cayenne pepper (more or less to desired spiciness)

1 teaspoon freshly ground black pepper

1 teaspoon kosher salt

1. In a medium bowl, mix all the ingredients until well combined.

2. Sprinkle the seasoning generously over grilled chicken, fish, or shrimp.

3. Store in an airtight container in a cool, dry place for up to 6 months.

Period 6
ON THE SIDELINE

BBQ SIDE DISHES

I'm a firm believer that side dishes can make or break the meal. This chapter includes my absolute favorite, showstopping sides, from my smoked bacon beans, which were always a sell-out on my BBQ rig, to my viral mac and cheese that garnered millions of views across social media. With these recipes at your disposal, you'll be the hero of any BBQ!

- Smack Slaw
- Big T's Smoked Mac and Cheese
- Smoked Bacon Beans
- Collard Greens
- Jalapeño Corn Bread
- Crunchy Broccoli Salad
- Hasselback Potatoes
- Mom-Mom Betty's Corn Pudding
- Donna's Pineapple Bake
- Grilled Mexican Street Corn

SMACK SLAW

SERVES 4

After a few bites of this creamy, tangy, and spicy slaw, I've converted even the most serious of coleslaw doubters. This recipe incorporates a kick of cayenne and sriracha, apple cider vinegar and mayo, the subtle sweetness of apple juice and sugar, and the depth of smoked paprika and garlic powder. With the addition of vibrant red cabbage and a pop of flavor from red onions, this coleslaw is colorful, enticing, and impossible to resist. Prepare to be SMACKED!

1 cup finely shredded green cabbage

1 cup finely shredded red cabbage

½ cup grated carrot

¼ cup thinly sliced red onion

¼ cup mayonnaise

2 tablespoons apple cider vinegar

2 tablespoons apple juice

1 tablespoon granulated sugar, plus more as needed

1 tablespoon sriracha sauce (more or less to desired spiciness)

¼ teaspoon cayenne pepper (more or less to desired spiciness)

½ teaspoon smoked paprika

½ teaspoon garlic powder

½ teaspoon kosher salt

¼ teaspoon freshly ground black pepper

Chopped fresh parsley or cilantro for garnish (optional)

1. In a large bowl, combine the green cabbage, red cabbage, carrot, and red onion. Toss together to mix evenly.

2. In a small bowl, prepare the dressing: Whisk together the mayonnaise, vinegar, apple juice, sugar, sriracha, cayenne, smoked paprika, garlic powder, salt, and pepper until well combined.

3. Pour the dressing over the shredded vegetables. Gently toss to coat all the ingredients thoroughly with the dressing.

4. Cover the bowl with plastic wrap and refrigerate for at least 1 hour before serving to allow the flavors to meld.

5. Just before serving, give the coleslaw a final toss and adjust the seasoning to your taste preference. Add more sriracha or cayenne for extra heat or a touch of sugar for added sweetness.

6. Garnish with parsley or cilantro, if desired, for a burst of freshness and color.

7. Serve as a delightful side dish to your favorite grilled meats or sandwiches, or as a topping for tacos or pulled pork. Enjoy the perfect balance of creaminess, tanginess, and spiciness in every mouthwatering bite!

CHEAT SHEET

- Make sure to wash and dry the vegetables thoroughly before shredding or chopping.

- Whether you're using a knife, mandoline, or food processor, try to shred the cabbage and other vegetables as evenly as possible. This ensures a consistent texture and helps the flavors to blend well.

- You want enough dressing to coat the vegetables thoroughly but not so much that it becomes soggy. You can always add more dressing as needed, so start with a conservative amount and adjust to taste.

BIG T'S SMOKED MAC AND CHEESE

SERVES 6

When I first began the journey of starting my own BBQ business, I sought out and surrounded myself with the experts. I was a sponge! One of my best friends, Terrance Williams, also known as Big T Will, was the first person I called. He ran a local BBQ spot for years out of an adjoining pizza shop. Some of the best BBQ around. When Big T Will invited me over and shared his mac and cheese recipe with me, I knew it was a game changer. However, as a true pitmaster, Terrance did not divulge ALL his secrets—to this day I still do not know three of his ingredients—but this version is my spin on his unbelievable recipe. The classic mac and cheese gets its velvety richness from Velveeta and is elevated by a blend of cheddar, nutty Parmesan, gooey mozzarella, and gouda cheese. This combination of cheeses adds an extra layer of flavor and creaminess, making it incredibly irresistible.

1 pound elbow macaroni

Cooking spray or butter, for greasing the pan

3 cups milk

½ teaspoon smoked paprika

1 teaspoon fresh cracked black pepper

1 tablespoon favorite BBQ rub

16 ounces Velveeta, cubed

4 tablespoons (½ stick) unsalted butter, cut into pieces

8 ounces cheddar cheese

8 ounces mozzarella cheese

1 cup grated Parmesan cheese

2 cups (12 ounces) gouda cheese

1. Preheat your smoker or grill to 275°F and prepare it for indirect heat cooking. If using a charcoal grill, place the coals on one side and leave the other side empty for the pan of mac and cheese.

2. Cook the macaroni according to the package instructions until al dente. Drain the cooked pasta and set it aside.

3. Shred all the cheeses and mix them together in a large bowl. You should end up with roughly 6 cups.

4. Grease a deep disposable aluminum half pan with spray or butter.

5. In a large saucepan, over medium heat, melt together the butter, Velveeta, 3 cups shredded cheese, and 2 cups milk. Stir together until smooth.

6. Place the noodles in an aluminum half pan. Mix in the parmesan cheese, granulated garlic, black pepper, 2 cups shredded cheese, and 1 cup milk. Mix thoroughly.

7. Pour the cheese sauce into the pan and stir well. Top with 1 cup of remaining shredded cheese and pour 1 cup of milk evenly across the top. Sprinkle on your favorite BBQ rub.

CHEAT SHEET

- You can add wood chips or pellets like hickory, mesquite, or applewood for different flavor profiles.

- Cook the pasta until it's just al dente or slightly undercooked. It will continue to cook when you bake the mac and cheese, so you want to avoid overcooking it and ending up with mushy pasta.

- Resting the smoked mac and cheese for a few minutes before serving allows the cheese to set slightly and makes it easier to scoop out servings without it collapsing.

8. Place the pan on the smoker over indirect heat and smoke for 30 to 45 minutes, until crust is brown and bubbly! Stir in ¾ each of the cheddar, mozzarella, and Parmesan cheeses, a little at a time, until all the cheeses are melted and the sauce is creamy and velvety. Season with salt and pepper.

9. Add the cooked elbow macaroni to the cheese sauce, stirring until the pasta is evenly coated with the creamy mixture.

10. Pour the mac and cheese into the prepared aluminum pan or cast-iron skillet and add remaining cheese on top.

11. Place the pan of mac and cheese on the side of the smoker or grill away from direct heat. Close the lid and let it smoke for about 1 hour, until the top develops a golden brown crust and the flavors are infused with the smoky goodness.

12. Remove the smoked mac and cheese from the grill and let it cool slightly.

13. Enjoy the combination of creamy cheese and smoky flavor that will leave everyone at the table smacking their lips!

SMOKED BACON BEANS

SERVES 8

I could not keep these smoked bacon beans on my menu for long before crossing them out with the SOLD OUT sign. I will start by saying canned beans are your friend—embrace them! Not only are they delicious, they are much easier than trying to do this from scratch. Once again, I have to give props to Kristin, minus the bacon! This is her recipe, and if you're a vegetarian, you can easily leave out the bacon for just-as-delicious vegetarian baked beans.

6 slices thick-cut bacon

1 yellow onion, chopped

2 (28-ounce) cans baked beans
(I use Bush's)

½ cup dark brown sugar

¼ cup apple cider vinegar

2 tablespoons yellow mustard

2 tablespoons ketchup

2 tablespoons molasses

1. Preheat your smoker to 250°F.

2. Start by cooking the bacon. I like to use a cast-iron skillet for this recipe, but you can use a casserole dish or even a disposable aluminum half pan. Cook the bacon on the stovetop over high heat for a few minutes on each side. You do not want the bacon crispy, but the fat should start to render. The bacon will finish in the smoker.

3. Remove the bacon from the pan and set aside. Add the onions to the bacon fat in the pan and cook for 5 minutes, or until soft and translucent.

4. Put the beans in your cast-iron pan, casserole dish, or aluminum half pan along with the brown sugar, vinegar, mustard, ketchup, and molasses and stir to incorporate fully.

5. Top the beans with your precooked slices of bacon, place on your smoker, and cook uncovered for 2 hours.

6. Remove the beans from the smoker, allow them to cool slightly (because they will be hot as molten lava!), and enjoy.

CHEAT SHEET

- Stir the beans occasionally while they're smoking to ensure even cooking and to prevent them from sticking to the bottom of the pan.

- Allow the smoked baked beans to rest for a few minutes before serving for the flavors to settle and the sauce to thicken slightly.

COLLARD GREENS

Kristin has a knack for making delicious collard greens. They are slowly simmered with bacon (optional if you're a vegetarian like her), onions, garlic, and a touch of vinegar to create a comforting dish that warms both the heart and the palate.

2 tablespoons extra virgin olive oil

1 large onion, chopped

4 cloves garlic, minced

4 slices bacon

4 cups chicken or vegetable broth

2 pounds collard greens, stemmed and chopped

¼ cup apple cider vinegar

1 teaspoon smoked paprika

½ teaspoon red pepper flakes (optional, for a hint of heat)

Kosher salt and freshly ground black pepper

1. In a large pot or Dutch oven, heat the oil over your grill's side burner or a stovetop.

2. Add the onion and garlic to the pot and cook until the onion becomes translucent and the garlic is fragrant.

3. Add the bacon slices to the pot and cook until crispy.

4. Pour in the broth and bring it to a simmer. Stir in the collard greens. Add the vinegar, smoked paprika and red pepper flakes (if using) and season with salt and black pepper.

5. Cover the pot and let the collard greens simmer on the grill's side burner or a stovetop for 1 to 1½ hours, until the greens are tender and infused with all the rich flavors.

CHEAT SHEET

- Look for fresh collard greens with crisp, vibrant leaves. Avoid greens with yellow or wilted leaves, as they may be past their prime.

- Collard greens can be gritty, so it's essential to wash them thoroughly. Submerge the leaves in a bowl of cold water and swish them around to remove any dirt or debris. Repeat until the water runs clear.

JALAPEÑO CORN BREAD

SERVES 8

Every BBQ needs corn bread. I'm not a huge spice guy, so I use jalapeños—which land on the milder side of the hot pepper family—to bring a balanced heat to the sweetness of the cornmeal. With the added flavors of cheddar cheese and creamy buttermilk, this recipe takes classic corn bread to the next level. Plus, you can enjoy it fresh off the grill or toasted the next day—it will be delicious either way!

1 cup cornmeal

1 cup all-purpose flour

¼ cup granulated sugar

1 tablespoon baking powder

½ teaspoon baking soda

½ teaspoon kosher salt

1 cup buttermilk

4 tablespoons (½ stick) unsalted butter, melted

2 large eggs, lightly beaten

1 cup grated cheddar cheese

2 to 3 jalapeño chiles, seeds removed and finely chopped (adjust to desired spiciness)

1. Preheat your grill to 350°F and grease a cast-iron skillet or grill-safe baking dish with butter or cooking spray.

2. In a large bowl, whisk together the cornmeal, flour, sugar, baking powder, baking soda, and salt.

3. In a separate bowl, mix together the buttermilk, butter, and lightly beaten eggs.

4. Pour the wet ingredients into the dry ingredients and stir until just combined.

5. Fold in the cheese and jalapeños, distributing them evenly throughout the batter.

6. Pour the batter into the prepared cast-iron skillet or baking dish, spreading it out evenly.

7. Place the skillet or baking dish on the grill and cover it with the grill's lid.

8. Bake for 25 to 30 minutes, until the top is golden brown and a toothpick inserted into the center comes out clean.

9. Remove the corn bread from the grill and let it cool slightly before serving.

CHEAT SHEET

- Adjust the amount of jalapeños you use based on your preference for spice. If you're sensitive to heat, you can use fewer jalapeños or remove the seeds and membranes to reduce the heat level.

- Jalapeño corn bread is best served warm, either on its own or with a pat of butter and a drizzle of honey for sweetness.

CRUNCHY BROCCOLI SALAD

SERVES 6

Every BBQ has to have some cold side dishes, and this crunchy, colorful broccoli salad is the one! Crisp broccoli florets, chewy cranberries, crunchy almonds, and a creamy dressing deliver a bite that is cool and refreshing and that will satisfy carnivores and vegetarians alike.

Kosher salt

4 cups broccoli florets, cut into bite-sized pieces

½ cup dried cranberries

¼ cup sliced almonds, toasted

¼ cup diced red onion

½ cup mayonnaise

2 tablespoons apple cider vinegar

1 tablespoon honey

1 teaspoon Dijon mustard

Freshly ground black pepper

1. Bring a big pot of water to a boil and season it heavily with salt, like you would for pasta water. If you taste a spoonful, it should taste as salty as the ocean.

2. Add the broccoli florets to the water and cook for 1 minute, or until bright green in color.

3. Immediately drain the broccoli florets, then rinse with cold water for 2 minutes, or until the broccoli has cooled down. This will stop the cooking process, leaving the broccoli crunchy but free of that unpleasant raw texture.

4. Transfer the broccoli to a salad spinner and spin the broccoli dry. Then blot dry further with a kitchen towel to prevent excess water from diluting the dressing.

5. In a large bowl, combine the broccoli florets, dried cranberries, sliced almonds, and red onion. Toss together to mix evenly.

6. In a small bowl, prepare the dressing: Whisk together the mayonnaise, vinegar, honey, and mustard until well combined. Season with salt and pepper.

7. Pour the dressing over the broccoli mixture. Gently toss to coat all the ingredients thoroughly with the creamy dressing.

8. Cover the bowl with plastic wrap and refrigerate for at least 30 minutes before serving to allow the flavors to meld.

9. Just before serving, give the broccoli salad a final toss and adjust the seasoning to your taste preference.

CHEAT SHEET

After tossing the broccoli with the dressing, marinate the salad in the refrigerator for at least 30 minutes to allow the flavors to meld together and for the broccoli to absorb the dressing.

HASSELBACK POTATOES

I love a good baked potato, but they can get boring. While the technique has been around for a long time, hasselback potatoes were reinvented on social media! The thin slices create a crispy crunch as well as a crevasse to soak up and hold all the flavor of the olive oil, garlic, herbs, and butter! A flavorful twist that not only looks cool but intensifies the flavor and texture of the potatoes.

4 large russet potatoes

4 tablespoons (½ stick) unsalted butter, melted

2 tablespoons extra virgin olive oil

4 cloves garlic, minced

1 tablespoon chopped fresh thyme leaves

1 tablespoon chopped fresh rosemary leaves

Salt and freshly ground black pepper

Grated Parmesan cheese, for garnish (optional)

Chopped fresh parsley, for garnish (optional)

1. Preheat your grill for indirect medium-high heat.

2. Scrub the russet potatoes clean and pat them dry. Place a potato between two chopsticks or wooden spoons parallel to one another. Make thin slices across the potatoes, cutting almost to the bottom but not all the way through, using the chopsticks or spoons as a guide to prevent cutting all the way through.

3. In a small bowl, mix together the melted butter, oil, garlic, thyme, and rosemary.

4. Place the sliced potatoes in a grill-safe baking dish or on a piece of aluminum foil.

5. Drizzle the butter and herb mixture over each potato, making sure to get it between the slices as much as possible. Season the potatoes with salt and pepper.

6. Cover the baking dish with aluminum foil and place on the indirect side of the grill. Close the lid and cook the potatoes for 40 to 50 minutes, until they are fork-tender.

7. Remove the aluminum foil from the potatoes and continue to grill them indirect for another 10 minutes, or until they are crispy and lightly browned on the edges.

8. If desired, sprinkle grated Parmesan cheese over the potatoes during the last 5 minutes of grilling to add an extra layer of savory goodness.

9. Remove the hasselback potatoes from the grill, let them cool slightly, top with parsley (if using), and serve.

CHEAT SHEET

- Soak the sliced potatoes in cold water for 30 minutes to remove excess starch. This helps them become crispy on the outside while remaining tender on the inside.

- Occasionally baste the potatoes with melted butter or oil while baking to keep them moist and flavorful.

MOM-MOM BETTY'S CORN PUDDING

SERVES 8

Kristin's Mom-Mom Betty wrote this recipe on the outside of an envelope in 1988, and it has been a constant at every family function since I met my wife almost fifteen years ago. The nostalgia of a recipe that has been passed down from generation to generation only adds to the experience, and I'm so excited to share a piece of Betty's love with you!

2½ cups milk

4 tablespoons (½ stick) unsalted butter

½ cup sugar

1 tablespoon kosher salt

½ cup cornstarch

2 cans whole corn, drained

2 cans creamed corn

4 large eggs

1. Preheat the oven to 400°F.

2. Lightly grease or butter a 9 x 13-inch casserole dish.

3. In a large pot, combine the milk, butter, sugar, salt, and cornstarch. Place over medium heat and whisk until well combined.

4. Stir in drained whole corn and creamed corn until fully incorporated. Cook, stirring, for 5 minutes, or until thickened.

5. Remove from the heat and let cool for a few minutes.

6. Whisk the eggs in a small bowl. Temper the egg mixture by mixing a small amount of the corn mixture into the eggs. Slowly add the rest of the corn mixture until the egg is thoroughly combined. Tempering gets the eggs to combine without cooking them.

7. Pour the mixture into the prepared casserole dish and bake for 1 hour, or until golden brown and crispy.

8. Remove from the oven and cool for a few minutes to allow it to set slightly and make it easier to slice before serving.

DONNA'S PINEAPPLE BAKE

SERVES 6 TO 8

Keeping it in the family, I had to call my mother-in-law for this pineapple bake recipe. Is it a side dish or is it a dessert? I will leave that for you to decide—regardless, it disappears every time.

1 cup (2 sticks) unsalted butter, at room temperature, plus more for the pan

2 cups sugar

1 tablespoon ground cinnamon

8 large eggs

10 slices white bread, torn into small pieces

Two 20-ounce cans crushed pineapple

1 can sliced pineapple rounds

1 can maraschino cherries

1. Preheat the oven to 350°F.

2. Lightly grease a 9 x 13-inch casserole dish.

3. Mix the butter, sugar, and 1½ teaspoons of the cinnamon together by hand in a large bowl or with a mixer. Add the eggs one at a time until incorporated and use a spatula to fold in the bread and crushed pineapple (don't forget the juice). Stir gently until it is all incorporated, then pour the mixture into the prepared casserole dish.

4. Sprinkle the remaining 1½ teaspoons cinnamon evenly over the top. Arrange the pineapple rounds on top and place a cherry in the center of each one.

5. Bake for 1 hour, or until lightly browned and bubbly.

6. Let the casserole cool for about 20 minutes before serving.

GRILLED MEXICAN STREET CORN

SERVES 6

The first time I ate grilled corn on the cob was in Columbus, Ohio, at my Aunt Norma's house. My aunt and uncle had a cornfield in the backyard, so corn—often grilled and slathered in butter—was on the table at almost every meal. This recipe, with the added flavors of tangy lime, creamy mayo, and spicy chili powder, takes me right back to their house.

6 ears corn

½ cup mayonnaise

¼ cup sour cream

½ cup crumbled cotija or feta cheese

1 teaspoon chili powder (more or less to desired spiciness)

¼ cup chopped fresh cilantro

1 lime, cut into 6 wedges

Salt and freshly ground black pepper

1. Preheat your grill to medium-high heat.

2. Gently peel back the husks of the corn but leave them attached at the bottom. Remove the silks, discard them, and cover the corn back up with the husk. Let the corn soak in cold water for 30 minutes.

3. Place the corn on the grill and cook for 10 to 15 minutes, turning occasionally, until the kernels are tender and slightly charred.

4. While the corn is grilling, in a small bowl, mix together the mayonnaise and sour cream until well combined.

5. In a separate small bowl, mix together the crumbled cheese and chili powder.

6. Remove the corn from the grill and let it cool slightly.

7. Brush each ear of corn with the mayo–sour cream mixture, coating all sides.

8. Sprinkle the chili powder–coated cotija cheese over each ear of corn, pressing it into the mayo–sour cream mixture to adhere.

9. Garnish the ears of corn with cilantro and finish with a squeeze of lime.

Period 7
SWEET TOOTH

DESSERTS

For a long time, baking was far from my comfort zone—but with no risk comes no reward! I'm most confident when I'm outside, at the grill, so it's no surprise that my go-to dessert recipes are creations from taking the baking out of the kitchen and firing up the barbecue. Over the years, I've gathered these decadent recipes from my culinary adventures, experimenting with some and receiving others from friends, neighbors, and mentors (full credit given). No meal is complete without a dessert to top it off, and when you can combine sweet flavors with the smoky char from the grill, you achieve a perfect balance!

- Corn Bread Cupcakes with Honey Butter Cream and Candied Bacon
- Smoked Berry Cobbler
- Banana Pudding
- BBQ Banana Split
- Smoked Apple Crisp
- Chocolate Dump Cake
- Sopapilla with Grilled Peaches and Hot Buttered Rum

CORN BREAD CUPCAKES WITH HONEY BUTTER CREAM AND CANDIED BACON

SERVES 15

Because I'm always experimenting with new recipes and cooking for large groups, I often end up with more food than even my hungry family can finish. So, I regularly gift plates of BBQ to my neighbors! Imagine knock-knock, zoom-zoom, or ding-dong ditch, but with a plate of delicious meats left behind. One day, my neighbor Lindsay returned the favor by leaving a tray of beautiful bacon-topped cupcakes at my doorstep. After dinner that night, I bit into one and was blown away by the perfection: corn bread! I immediately recruited Lindsay to make these corn bread cupcakes for my BBQ truck, and we never looked back. From the first day on my rig, they sold out.

For the Corn Bread Cupcakes:

1⅓ cups all-purpose flour

⅓ cup yellow cornmeal

½ teaspoon baking powder

¼ teaspoon baking soda

¼ teaspoon salt

½ cup (1 stick) unsalted butter, softened

½ cup honey

½ cup sugar

2 large eggs

½ cup milk

¼ cup sour cream

½ teaspoon vanilla extract

1. Make the cupcakes: Preheat the oven to 350°F and line a cupcake tin with paper liners.

2. In a medium bowl, combine the flour, cornmeal, baking powder, baking soda, and salt.

3. In a large bowl using an electric mixer, beat the butter, honey, and sugar until the mixture becomes light and fluffy, about 2 minutes. Beat in the eggs one at a time. Add the wet ingredients along with half of the dry ingredients and mix until almost fully combined. Add the remaining dry ingredients and mix until well combined.

4. Divide the batter evenly among the cupcake liners about two-thirds full. Bake for 18 to 20 minutes, until a toothpick comes out clean. (Increase the oven temperature to 400ºF to get it ready for the bacon.) Let the cupcakes cool in the tins for 5 minutes, then remove them and place on a wire rack to cool completely.

5. As the cupcakes cool, make the honey butter cream: In

For the Honey Butter Cream:

⅓ cup milk, plus more if needed

2 tablespoons heavy cream

2 tablespoons all-purpose flour

½ cup (1 stick) unsalted butter, softened

2 tablespoons honey

1 cup powdered sugar, plus more if needed

Pinch of salt

For the Candied Bacon:

¼ cup brown sugar

¼ teaspoon cayenne pepper

12 strips bacon

a small saucepan, whisk the milk, cream, and flour over medium heat until it thickens, 4 to 5 minutes. Remove from the heat, pour into a shallow bowl, place in the freezer, and leave for about 15 minutes, until the mixture is room temperature.

6. While the flour mixture is cooling, using an electric mixer, beat the butter for 2 minutes on medium speed. Add the honey and powdered sugar and mix until light and fluffy. Add the cooled cooked mixture a little at a time while mixing and beat until fully combined. If needed, add a little milk a tablespoon at a time to thin or powdered sugar to thicken.

7. Make the candied bacon: Combine the brown sugar and cayenne in a small bowl. Line a baking sheet with parchment paper or aluminum foil or spray with cooking spray. Layer the bacon on the prepared sheet and sprinkle the brown sugar mixture over the bacon. Bake until crispy, about 10 minutes. Let cool on the pan for 15 minutes, then chop into small pieces.

8. Pipe the honey butter cream onto the cooled cupcakes and sprinkle with candied bacon.

CHEAT SHEET

Cooking whole slices of bacon gives you more creative freedom for their presentation. You can cut them into 1-inch squares or chop them into a bacon crumble. Regardless of what you choose, your cupcake topping will be delicious.

SMOKED BERRY COBBLER

This cobbler is the perfect summertime BBQ dessert. The trifecta of berries, married with a tender, golden crust and a kiss of smoke—there's really nothing like it. Plus, thanks to the very simple batter and quick cook time, this is the perfect amount of "baking" for me.

4 cups mixed berries (such as strawberries, blueberries, and raspberries)

1½ cups granulated sugar

1 tablespoon lemon juice

1 cup all-purpose flour

1 teaspoon baking powder

½ teaspoon salt

1 cup milk

½ cup (1 stick) unsalted butter, melted

Vanilla ice cream, for serving

1. Preheat your smoker to 350°F. Grease a grill-safe baking dish.

2. In a large bowl, gently toss the berries with ½ cup of the sugar and the lemon juice. Allow them to macerate while you prepare the batter. Macerating gives the berries time to extract their natural sweetness, resulting in a cobbler with tender, juicy berries and lots of juicy syrup.

3. Whisk together the flour, remaining 1 cup sugar, baking powder, and salt in another bowl. Stir in the milk and melted butter until the batter is smooth.

4. Pour the batter into the prepared baking dish. Spoon the macerated berries evenly over the batter.

5. Place the baking dish in the smoker and bake for 30 to 35 minutes, until the topping is golden and the berries are bubbling.

6. Remove from the smoker and let cool slightly. Serve warm with a scoop of vanilla ice cream.

CHEAT SHEET

- I like to make my cobblers (and many other things) in a cast-iron pan. Not only does it look awesome, it's the best pan for getting those sweet, caramelized, crunchy edges.

- Once you've perfected this recipe, try it with other fruits, such as peaches or apples.

BANANA PUDDING

Comfort food doesn't typically come in the form of a chewy, creamy, and cool dessert. Banana pudding, however, does. There are all types of banana puddings, but this recipe is a great place to start. It's simple, delicious, and easy to modify to make it your own.

¾ cup sugar

¼ cup all-purpose flour

⅛ teaspoon salt

1 whole large egg

3 cups milk

4 large egg yolks

1 teaspoon vanilla extract

4 ripe but firm bananas

1 tablespoon fresh lemon juice

40 Nilla Wafers

Whipped cream and banana
slices, for serving (optional)

1. Combine the sugar, flour, salt, whole egg, and milk in a large saucepan. Whisk well. Add the egg yolks and whisk until smooth.

2. Cook over medium-low heat, stirring frequently, until thickened, about 15 minutes. Turn off the heat and stir in the vanilla.

3. Peel 2 of the bananas and slice them into ¼-inch-thick rounds. Place them in a large bowl, add the lemon juice, and toss to coat.

4. Line the bottom of a 9 x 13-inch casserole dish with 30 of the Nilla Wafers. Arrange the sliced bananas evenly over the wafers. Do this just before the pudding is finished so they don't brown. Add half of the pudding in an even layer.

5. Peel and slice the remaining 2 bananas and layer them over the pudding. Pour the rest of the pudding over the bananas.

6. Crush the remaining 10 Nilla Wafers and sprinkle them over the top of the pudding.

7. Cover and refrigerate for at least 4 hours to allow flavors to meld and for the pudding to set properly.

8. Serve topped with whipped cream and banana slices, if you like.

CHEAT SHEET

- Make sure your bananas are ripe but not mushy. You want them to have a sweet flavor and a firm texture that holds up in the pudding.

- While you can use instant pudding mix, making pudding from scratch gives a richer flavor and creamier texture. It's not difficult and definitely worth the effort.

BBQ BANANA SPLIT

SERVES 4

When I was a kid, and even now, when I hear that familiar tune of Mister Softee from around the corner, the first thing I think of is a banana split. It was a huge treat when my dad would let me get one. Now as a dad myself, I can bring that nostalgia to my kids! This recipe is a perfect way to involve the whole family—Aidric and Nash love loading up the grilled bananas with their favorite toppings and sauces before diving in!

¼ cup brown sugar

1 teaspoon ground cinnamon

4 ripe bananas (unpeeled)

1. Preheat your grill to medium heat.

2. In a small bowl, mix the brown sugar and cinnamon.

Vanilla ice cream

Chocolate sauce

Caramel sauce

Whipped cream

1 cup chopped walnuts

4 maraschino cherries

3. Leaving the peel on, cut each banana in half lengthwise.

4. Sprinkle the bananas with the brown sugar–cinnamon mixture and grill peel-side down for about 5 minutes, until the topping is melted. Flip and grill banana-side down for 30 seconds for a little extra caramelization. Watch carefully here, as the sugar can burn quickly.

5. Remove the bananas from the grill and let them cool slightly.

6. Gently peel back the skin, leaving the bananas intact. Place each grilled banana in a dish and top with ice cream.

7. Drizzle with chocolate sauce and caramel sauce, then add whipped cream, nuts, and a cherry on top.

CHEAT SHEET

Leaving the peel on the banana while grilling helps prevent the sugars from burning during the cook!

SMOKED APPLE CRISP

SERVES 6

One of the most memorable flavors of my childhood was my Nan's apple pie. The days leading up to her visit were filled with anticipation, imagining the sugary crunch of the pie crust combined with the gooey, tender apple filling. This recipe is inspired by those memories, with a BBQ twist: some sweet applewood smoke!

4 apples, peeled, cored, and sliced

2 tablespoons lemon juice

¼ cup granulated sugar

1 teaspoon ground cinnamon

1 cup old-fashioned oats

½ cup all-purpose flour

½ cup brown sugar

½ cup (1 stick) cold unsalted butter, cubed

Vanilla ice cream, for serving

1. Prepare your grill or smoker for indirect heat with applewood at 300°F.

2. In a large bowl, toss the apple slices with the lemon juice, granulated sugar, and cinnamon.

3. In a separate large bowl, combine oats, flour, and brown sugar. Cut in the butter until the mixture resembles coarse crumbs.

4. Place the apple slices in a grill-safe baking dish. Sprinkle the oat mixture evenly over the apples.

5. Grill the apple crisp for 25 to 30 minutes, until the apples are tender and the topping is golden brown. Remove from the grill and let cool slightly.

6. Serve warm with a scoop of vanilla ice cream.

CHEAT SHEET

- Slice the apples evenly so they cook uniformly, avoiding undercooked and overly soft slices. Aim for slices that are 1/4 to 1/2 inch thick.

- For extra crunch and flavor, consider adding chopped nuts such as pecans or walnuts to the topping mixture.

CHOCOLATE DUMP CAKE

Four ingredients, a couple steps, and a smoker! This is a simple chocolate dump cake, but the smoker takes it to a whole different gooey, chocolaty level. As it cooks, layers form, textures meld, and the result is an irresistible dessert that's as easy to make as it is addictive.

One 21-ounce can cherry pie filling

1 box chocolate cake mix

½ cup (1 stick) unsalted butter, melted

½ cup chocolate chips

Vanilla ice cream, for serving (optional)

1. Preheat your smoker to 300°F for indirect heat using your choice of wood.

2. Spread the cherry pie filling evenly over a grill-safe baking dish. Sprinkle the chocolate cake mix over the pie filling. Drizzle the melted butter over the cake mix, then scatter the chocolate chips on top.

3. Grill the cake indirectly for 30 to 40 minutes, until the cake is cooked through, the cherry filling is bubbly, and the top is golden brown and crisp. If you insert a toothpick into the center, it should come out clean or with a few moist crumbs attached.

4. Remove from the grill and allow it to cool for 10 minutes.

5. Serve warm, with or without a scoop of vanilla ice cream.

CHEAT SHEET

Because dump cakes are known for their simplicity, using quality ingredients can make a big difference in flavor. Opt for high-quality chocolate cake mix and cocoa powder and real butter for the best results.

SOPAPILLA WITH GRILLED PEACHES AND HOT BUTTERED RUM

SERVES 12

Every family has a go-to restaurant—ours is Holy Tomato in Blackwood, New Jersey. Not only do they have some of the best pizza you will ever have, but their homemade sopapilla cheesecake is easily in my top three all-time desserts. Because we can't go out to eat every night, I figured I would take a shot at re-creating it at home—but with a little twist on the grill. The grilled peaches and hot buttered rum sauce take it from my top three to NUMBER ONE!

For the Sopapilla:

Cooking spray

Two 8-ounce packs cream cheese, softened

1¾ cups sugar

1 teaspoon vanilla extract

2 cans Pillsbury Crescent Rolls

½ cup (1 stick) unsalted butter, softened

1 teaspoon ground cinnamon

For the Peaches and Hot Buttered Rum:

¼ cup brown sugar

4 tablespoons (½ stick) unsalted butter

½ teaspoon ground cinnamon

¼ teaspoon salt

¼ cup rum

4 ripe peaches, pitted and sliced

1. Preheat the oven to 350°F and grease a 9 x 13-inch baking dish with cooking spray.

2. Using a hand mixer, beat together the cream cheese, 1 cup of the granulated sugar, and the vanilla until smooth.

3. Unroll the crescent roll dough without separating the triangles and use a rolling pin to flatten it to fit into the baking dish.

4. Spread the cream cheese mixture on top of the crescent dough, then cover with the second can of crescent dough rolled out the same way as the first.

5. In a small bowl, combine the remaining ¾ cup granulated sugar, the butter, and the cinnamon and, using a fork, mash together until fully incorporated. Arrange tablespoons of the mixture over the top of the dough.

6. Preheat your grill to high heat. You want a ripping-hot grill to char the peaches without letting them get soft and mushy.

7. In a medium pot, combine brown sugar, butter, cinnamon, salt, and rum. Mix well and bring to a boil over medium-

CHEAT SHEET

- Bake the cheesecake until the top layer of crescent roll dough is golden brown and the cheesecake filling is set. It's okay if the center is slightly jiggly—it will continue to set as it cools.

- For best results, chill the cheesecake in the refrigerator for a few hours or overnight before serving. This allows the flavors to meld together and results in a firmer texture.

high heat. Turn down the heat to low and simmer until the sauce reduces to a glaze-like consistency.

8. While the sauce simmers, pit the peaches and slice them into 6 wedges each. Place the wedges on the grill and do not touch them. Once they begin to char, the natural juices will begin to caramelize, and they will voluntarily release from the grill. If you mess with them too soon, they will stick. Once they release, flip and char the other side. Remove from the grill and set aside.

9. After 30 minutes, remove the sopapilla from the grill, let cool completely, then slice into 12 squares. This is a dessert I like to serve at room temperature, if not refrigerator-chilled.

10. Top each square with a few peaches and drizzle with the hot buttered rum sauce.

EXTRACURRICULAR ACTIVITIES

TAILGATING AND CAMPING

One morning in 2023, I was getting ready for school and saw a text from a colleague asking if I watched the Emmy-nominated *Kelce* documentary. It had just premiered the night before, so my answer was no, but she immediately told me to fast-forward to minute fifty-two and watch. So I did! Front and center on the screen, there I was, in all my tailgating glory! My favorite team, my favorite pastime, and doing my favorite activity. My fifteen minutes of fame!

It's fitting that my fifteen minutes of fame featured me grilling at a tailgate, because that's really how I got into this business in the first place. And when I wasn't tailgating, I was camping, which is kind of just like tailgating, but in the woods!

I've included a few tailgating and camping recipes in previous chapters, but I wanted to dedicate a section to my staples. Some of the biggest draws tailgating and grilling had for me were the comradery and sense of community—two elements that are also the backbone of BBQ. As you make these recipes, I hope you feel that, too!

- Smoked Bacon-Wrapped Scallops
- Bacon, Egg, and Cheese with Homemade English Muffins
- Backyard Jersey Cheesesteak
- Smoked Pig Shots
- Shrimp and Sausage Skewers
- Campfire S'mores Dip
- Grilled Sausage and Pepper Sammy
- Prosciutto-Wrapped Brie
- Smoked Buffalo Chicken Dip
- Beef Tallow Campfire Fries

SMOKED BACON-WRAPPED SCALLOPS

SERVES 4

Every single tailgate at Lincoln Financial Field (home of the Eagles) had bacon-wrapped scallops on the menu. They became my dad's second-favorite tailgate food (if you want to check out his first favorite, skip to page 202). When I started out, I would simply wrap the scallops in bacon, throw them on the grill, and pray that I cooked them enough without burning the bacon. Over time, my technique improved—especially when I started smoking them and adding a gentle slather of BBQ sauce. Tailgate victory!

12 large sea scallops

1 tablespoon extra virgin olive oil

2 tablespoons All-Purpose BBQ Rub (page 150)

6 slices bacon, halved crosswise

¼ cup Classic Sweet BBQ Sauce (page 147)

1. Preheat your smoker to 250°F.

2. Pat the scallops dry. Place them in a bowl and coat them with the oil and then the rub.

3. Precook the bacon before wrapping it around the scallops by pan-frying or baking it until it is partially cooked but still pliable.

4. Wrap each scallop with a half piece of bacon and secure with a toothpick.

5. Place the bacon-wrapped scallops on the smoker and cook for 30 minutes. I like to place the scallops on a baking rack for easier transportation.

6. After 30 minutes, brush the scallops with the BBQ sauce and continue to cook for another 10 minutes, or until the sauce is set, the bacon is cooked, and the scallops have an internal temperature of 145°F.

7. Remove from the smoker and serve.

CHEAT SHEET

Opt for thick-cut bacon slices, as they will hold their shape better during smoking and provide a satisfying meaty texture. Thin bacon slices may overcook or become too crispy before the scallops are done.

BACON, EGG, AND CHEESE WITH HOMEMADE ENGLISH MUFFINS

SERVES 6

Back to the tailgates and my dad's absolute favorite tailgate food! All the years I spent making bacon, egg, and cheese sandwiches in parking lots, I never knew how much I was missing two major ingredients: thick-cut bacon and homemade English muffins. I would usually grab the cheapest bacon, which was super thin, and the most famous store-bought English muffins in the land. It was always good, but we are talking next level here. So, now we make the easiest scratch English muffins ever and get that thick-cut bacon for the ultimate bacon, egg, and cheese!

For the English Muffins:

¾ cup milk

½ cup water

2 tablespoons sugar

2¼ teaspoons (1 packet) instant or fast-acting yeast

2¾ cups all-purpose flour

1 teaspoon kosher salt

1 egg large, at room temperature

3 tablespoons unsalted butter, melted

Oil, for the bowl

Cornmeal or semolina, for dusting

For the Bacon and Eggs:

12 slices thick-cut bacon

Oil, for frying

6 eggs

Softened butter

12 cheese slices (there's nothing like classic yellow American)

Kosher salt and freshly cracked black pepper

1. Start with the English muffins. Combine the milk, water, and sugar in a medium bowl or glass measuring cup. Stir together, then warm in the microwave to 110°F. Add the yeast and stir once more. Set aside for 5 to 7 minutes, until a foamy head develops.

2. While the yeast wakes up, combine the flour and salt in the bowl of your mixer and whisk together, then fit with a paddle attachment.

3. Mix the egg and melted butter into the milk mixture, then slowly pour the liquid into the flour mixture while mixing on low. Increase the speed to medium-high and mix for about 7 minutes, until the dough is elastic and smooth.

4. Oil a large bowl. Transfer the dough to the bowl and cover with plastic. Leave in a warm spot to double in size, about 1 hour.

5. Transfer the dough to a floured counter, then gently spread out and pat down until it's just under 1 inch thick. Line 2 baking sheets with parchment paper and sprinkle with cornmeal.

6. Use a 3-inch round cutter to cut your muffins, then transfer them to the baking sheets. Reroll the scraps and continue cutting until the dough is used up. Cover loosely with plastic wrap and place in a warm spot to rise for about 30 minutes.

7. Place a large skillet over very low heat. Once you can feel the heat when placing your hand a few inches over the surface, sprinkle with cornmeal, then carefully place 3 English muffins on the pan. Cover and cook for 5 to 6 minutes. Carefully flip and cook for another 5 to 6 minutes.

8. Clear the old cornmeal off the pan, add a fresh sprinkle, and cook the 3 remaining English muffins.

9. Preheat your grill to medium heat.

10. Cook the bacon on the grill until crispy.

11. Place a frying pan on the grill and fry the eggs to your liking.

12. Slice the English muffins and toast them on the grill. Butter the English muffins.

13. Assemble the sandwiches by layering on a fried egg, 2 bacon slices, and 2 cheese slices.

14. Season with salt and pepper and serve.

CHEAT SHEET

- Although you can let the dough proof for just 1 hour, the English muffins will have more flavor the longer you leave it (up to 4 to 8 hours).

- I recommend using a stand mixer to make these, as the dough is very sticky and difficult to handle.

- For storage: Cooked English muffins will keep well in an airtight container for 3 to 5 days or can be frozen for up to 3 months.

BACKYARD JERSEY CHEESESTEAK

SERVES 4

Born and raised in South Jersey, my entire family are die-hard Philadelphia sports fans! And along with being a Philadelphia fan comes the commitment and all-out loyalty to the Philadelphia cheesesteak. I have tried them all, some excellent and some downright disappointing. Regardless, I will always stand by my claim that the best "Philadelphia" cheesesteak actually comes from my backyard in Jersey! I only use ribeye steak, and please, for the love of all that is holy, a Philly cheesesteak *does not* have peppers. Provolone is acceptable, but the new king of the block in Philly is Cooper Sharp American if you can get it! Welcome to Philly!

4 hoagie rolls

1 large sweet onion, thinly sliced or diced

1 pound ribeye steak, thinly sliced

2 tablespoons unsalted butter, softened

2 cloves garlic, pressed

2 tablespoons extra virgin olive oil

½ teaspoon sea salt, or to taste

½ teaspoon freshly cracked black pepper, or to taste

8 slices provolone or Cooper Sharp American cheese

1. Preheat a griddle or large skillet over medium heat.

2. Slice the hoagie rolls three-quarters of the way through, thinly slice or dice the onions, and thinly slice the beef. Placing your beef in the freezer for 30 minutes will make it easier to get your slices thin.

3. Make a compound butter by combining the softened butter with the garlic. Mix well to incorporate the garlic into the butter. Spread the garlic butter on each side of the rolls. Place on the griddle and toast until golden brown. Remove from the griddle and set aside.

4. Add 1 tablespoon of the oil to the griddle, add the onions, and cook, stirring, until caramelized. Transfer to a bowl and set aside.

5. Add the remaining tablespoon of oil. Increase the heat to high and spread the sliced ribeye in an even layer on the griddle. Let it brown for a few minutes, then flip and season with salt and pepper. Cook until the steak is fully cooked through, then immediately stir in the caramelized onions.

6. This is where we get a little technical! Place the cheese over the top of the entire steak and onion mixture, and as it melts, mix it throughout the steak. You want an extremely evenly distributed cheese to steak ratio.

7. Divide the steak and onions into 4 equal portions and place the split rolls over the top of each portion for 1 minute.

8. Using a large spatula, scrape the cheesesteak into the bun as you flip it over, and you are left with the most perfect "Jersey" Philly cheesesteak even the most rowdy and critical Philadelphia fan would be proud of!

CHEAT SHEET

The roll makes the sandwich! Philly cheesesteaks are known for the rolls, so don't settle for any old grocery store rolls. Get freshly baked rolls and the sandwich will be significantly better. Seeded or not seeded is up to you.

SMOKED PIG SHOTS

SERVES 8

To say these smoked pig shots are the most requested thing I make would be an understatement. I have presented some version of them at events and festivals across the country, and they are always a crowd-pleaser. From Robert Irvine to Antonia Lofaso, they are chef approved! They have just the right amount of spice to go perfectly with the crisp bacon, smoky sausage, and cheesy, creamy filling. Take these on a test run with your friends and family, and I promise it will not be your last time making them!

8 ounces cream cheese, softened

5 jalapeño chiles, diced

2½ cups shredded cheddar cheese

5 tablespoons RubCity Groark Boys BBQ for Pork Rub or another seasoning

2½ pounds smoked sausage

2½ pounds thick-cut bacon

1. Preheat your smoker or grill to 350°F.

2. Mix the cream cheese, jalapeños, cheese, and rub in a medium bowl and set aside.

3. Slice the smoked sausage into 1-inch rounds. Cut the bacon strips in half.

4. Wrap each round of sausage with bacon, creating a cup that will hold the filling. Secure with a toothpick.

5. Fill the cup with the cream cheese mixture and sprinkle a little of the rub on top.

6. Place the pig shots on your smoker and cook until the bacon is rendered and crispy, 45 minutes to 1 hour.

7. Remove the pig shots from the smoker, let cool for about 10 minutes, and serve.

CHEAT SHEET

If you choose to use raw sausage, partially precook it by grilling, baking, or pan-frying before assembling the pig shots. This will ensure that it cooks through evenly while smoking.

SHRIMP AND SAUSAGE SKEWERS

SERVES 6 TO 8

Smoked sausage and shrimp is one of my favorite land-and-sea combinations. Typically, you see this combo in a dish like gumbo, but in this recipe, we're taking it to the campfire or the tailgate in the form of a simple grilled surf-and-turf skewer.

1 pound 16/20 count raw jumbo shrimp, peeled and deveined

2 teaspoons extra virgin olive oil

2 tablespoons Blackened Cajun Seasoning (page 152)

8 ounces andouille smoked sausage links (kielbasa also works well)

Special equipment: 6 to 8 wooden or metal skewers

1. Preheat your grill to medium-high heat.

2. If using wooden skewers, soak them in water for at least 30 minutes to prevent burning.

3. Pat the shrimp with paper towels. Place them in a large bowl, add the oil and 1 tablespoon of the Cajun seasoning, and toss to coat.

4. Slice the sausage to the same thickness as the shrimp, then tuck the sausage into the inside curve of the shrimp. It will fit nice and snug! I typically fit 3 or 4 shrimp and sausage bites on each skewer.

5. Grill for 2 minutes per side, or until the shrimp is opaque and cooked through. Since the sausage is already smoked, focus on getting some grill marks and not overcooking the shrimp.

6. Remove from grill, let cool for a few minutes, then serve.

CHEAT SHEET

The larger the shrimp, the better, to give you more room to tuck the sausage in between the head and tail of the shrimp.

CAMPFIRE S'MORES DIP

SERVES 8

S'mores are one of my boys' favorite desserts. What could be better than chocolate and marshmallow sandwiched between two graham crackers? This recipe is a twist on the campfire classic—and according to Aidric and Nash, even better than the original. The cast-iron pan is the perfect vehicle for layers of graham crackers, chocolate, and marshmallow goodness.

1 box graham crackers (you will need plenty for dipping)

1½ cups milk chocolate chips

12 large marshmallows (mini marshmallows work fine, too)

1. Preheat your grill for indirect cooking with one side on high heat and the other side off.

2. Line a cast-iron skillet with graham crackers, arrange the chocolate chips on top, and then layer on the marshmallows.

3. Place the skillet on the side with no heat. Close the grill and cook for 15 to 25 minutes.

4. No one knows your grill better than you—I recommend taking a look every 10 to 15 minutes. The s'mores are ready when the marshmallows turn golden and the chocolate is melted. Please be careful and use oven mitts—it will be hot!

5. Let cool for a few minutes and enjoy with extra graham crackers.

CHEAT SHEET

Get creative with your s'mores by experimenting with different types of chocolate, flavored marshmallows, or alternative fillings like peanut butter, caramel, or sliced strawberries. The possibilities are endless, so feel free to mix and match to create your perfect combination.

CHEAT SHEET

There would be nothing wrong with melting a nice
provolone cheese over the sausage and peppers
just before building your sandwiches!

GRILLED SAUSAGE AND PEPPER SAMMY

SERVES 4

Next to the infamous Philly cheesesteak, it doesn't get much better than a properly grilled sausage and pepper sandwich. I make sure to get a really nice char on the sausage to not only add flavor but to get that proper snap. I use a foil boat to finish the sausage over a bed of peppers and onions before stuffing it all in a soft and chewy roll.

8 links Italian sausage (sweet or hot is up to you!)

2 large sweet yellow onions

2 red bell peppers

2 green bell peppers

2 yellow bell peppers

Kosher salt and freshly ground black pepper

4 club rolls, split

1. If using a gas grill, turn the burners on one side to high. If using a charcoal grill, pile the coals on one side of the grill.

2. Place the sausage directly over the fire and cook, turning, until nicely charred and browned on all sides. Remove from the grill and set aside.

3. Peel the onions, cut them in half, and thinly slice them crosswise.

4. Cut the peppers in half, remove the stems and seeds, and slice them into thin strips.

5. Fold a large sheet of foil on all four sides to create a boat. Place the peppers and onions in the foil boat, season with salt and pepper, then place the grilled sausages on top.

6. Place the foil boat with sausage, peppers, and onions to the side of the grill with no fire, cover the grill, and cook for about 20 minutes, until the peppers and onions are softened, the sausage is fully cooked, and the juices run clear.

7. Slice the club rolls open and place 2 links of sausage in each roll. Cover with a healthy portion of peppers and onions and, quite honestly, there's nothing better to wash it down with than a cold beer!

PROSCIUTTO-WRAPPED BRIE

When it comes to the saying "You can never have too much of a good thing," cheese immediately comes to mind. Now wrap that cheese in prosciutto and you've got something truly magical! Serve it alongside some toasted bread points and a slice of tart Granny Smith apple for a salty, creamy appetizer that I promise you will be asked to make again and again.

6 to 8 slices prosciutto

1 wheel Brie cheese

2 tablespoons RubCity Groark Boys BBQ for Pork Rub or another rub

1 baguette

2 Granny Smith apples

1. Preheat your smoker to 275°F.

2. Wrap the slices of prosciutto around the cheese, making sure all sides, top, and bottom are covered.

3. Once the wheel of cheese is completely covered with prosciutto, season with the rub.

4. Place on the smoker and cook for 45 minutes to 1 hour, until prosciutto is nice and crispy. To best fuse the ingredients and keep the shape, put the side of the wheel of Brie where all the prosciutto ends meet directly on the grill grate.

5. Pull the cheese and let it rest for 5 minutes.

6. While cheese is resting, slice and toast the baguette and slice the apples.

7. Slice the wheel into quarter portions and serve with the baguette and apple slices.

CHEAT SHEET

Chill the wrapped Brie in the refrigerator for 15 to 30 minutes before smoking to make it easier to handle. This also helps the prosciutto hold its shape and prevents it from overcooking.

SMOKED BUFFALO CHICKEN DIP

There's always a lot going on at a tailgate, so I'm all about recipes that I can prep a day or two in advance and then easily reheat or smoke on site. This classic dip fits the bill perfectly. You can enjoy it with tortilla chips, use it to make sliders, or even by the spoonful. Whatever you decide to do, you'll be thanking me!

2 cups shredded cooked chicken (I like to use my Applewood Smoked Beer Can Chicken on page 85, but a store-bought rotisserie works great, too)

Two 8-ounce packages cream cheese, softened

½ cup ranch dressing

¾ cup Frank's RedHot Sauce, plus more to taste

1½ cups cheddar cheese

Sweet and Spicy Pork Rub (page 150) or another BBQ seasoning

1. Preheat your smoker to 250°F.

2. Place all your ingredients in a 9 x 13-inch disposable aluminum pan or a 12-inch cast-iron pan and mix everything together.

3. Place the pan onto the smoker and cook uncovered for about 1 hour, giving it a nice stir every 20 minutes.

4. Before taking the dip off the smoker, make sure to give it a taste test. If you think it should be spicier, add more Frank's RedHot.

5. When the cheese looks fully melted and everything is well combined, remove it from the smoker and give it one final stir. I like to enjoy the dip with tortilla chips, but do not sleep on making some mini buffalo chicken sliders!

BEEF TALLOW CAMPFIRE FRIES

Like most kids, Aidric and Nash love themselves some crispy french fries! With as much camping as we do, I figured why not take a shot at making some french fries over the firepit. These are easy to make and best served in the great outdoors—all you need is a firepit, a nice cast-iron Dutch oven, and some beef tallow and you'll be ready to rock!

4 large russet potatoes

1 cup Wagyu beef tallow (or vegetable oil, if you must!)

Salt

Ketchup, mayonnaise, or other dipping sauces for serving (optional)

1. Scrub the potatoes thoroughly under running water to remove any dirt. Pat them dry with a clean kitchen towel.

2. I prefer to leave the skin on my potatoes for added texture, but you can peel them if you prefer. Cut the potatoes into strips about ¼ inch thick.

3. Soak the potato slices in a bowl filled with cold water for about 30 minutes. This removes excess starch, resulting in crispier fries.

4. Build a campfire and let it burn down until you have a bed of hot coals. You'll need a steady, medium-high heat for cooking the fries.

5. In a cast-iron skillet or Dutch oven, melt the beef tallow over the campfire until it is hot and shimmering. The oil should read 375°F on an instant-read thermometer.

6. Carefully add the potato slices to the hot tallow, making sure not to overcrowd the pan. Add them in batches if necessary.

7. Cook the fries until they are golden brown and crisp, flipping them occasionally for even cooking, 5 to 7 minutes.

8. Once the fries are cooked to your desired level of crispiness, use a slotted spoon or tongs to transfer them to a plate lined with paper towels to drain any excess oil.

9. Season the fries with salt immediately, while they are still hot. Adjust the seasoning to your taste.

10. Serve with your favorite dipping sauces.

CHEAT SHEET

Always exercise caution when cooking over an open flame and with hot oil. Make sure you have proper fire safety equipment nearby.

EXTRA CREDIT

VEGETARIAN GRILLING

My wife, Kristin, has been a strict vegetarian for nearly her entire life. Given she's been married to me—the Meat Teacher—for over twelve years, I forgive you for assuming our opposing dietary preferences would've sparked some fiery debate.

People are constantly asking us how we're able to manage our dinners as a family when we are part carnivore and part vegetarian. And although I have a lot of fun joking about it on social media, there are two simple facts that make it very easy for us and households like ours. First, I love vegetables, and preparing them on a grill makes them even more delicious. Second, so many vegetarian dishes can be modified by simply adding a protein. For example, when I make the Stuffed Portobello Mushrooms (page 224), I often add some shredded chicken or pork to the mixture!

This section is dedicated to Kristin—she's inspired me to push my creativity on the grill to new heights. These vegetarian recipes are our family favorites, the ones I grill up most often for Kristin and the boys. Lots of them are naturally high in protein, but if you're in the mood for meat, they're easy to modify to add whatever you're craving!

- Stuffed Portobello Mushrooms
- Grilled Cauliflower Steak
- Corn Ribs
- Grilled Eggplant with Feta Salsa
- Grilled Guacamole
- Sweet and Spicy Grilled Sweet Potato Wedges
- Soy and Ginger–Marinated Grilled Tofu
- Fire-Roasted Bruschetta
- Smoked Spinach and Artichoke Dip
- Coffee-Rubbed Smoked Cream Cheese

STUFFED PORTOBELLO MUSHROOMS

SERVES 4

In the vegetarian world, portobello mushrooms are commonly used as a steak alternative because of their meaty texture. Years ago, I surprised Kristin with a dinner at a restaurant in Philly named Vedge, renowned for their innovative vegan menu. This recipe is inspired by the portobello mushrooms from that dinner. But because my wife isn't vegan, I went ahead and added a cheesy twist to the veggie filling.

- 4 portobello mushrooms
- 2 tablespoons plus 1 teaspoon extra virgin olive oil
- ½ yellow onion, finely diced
- 2 cloves garlic, minced
- ¼ cup finely diced red bell pepper
- 4 ounces cream cheese, softened
- ¼ cup sour cream
- 5 ounces frozen chopped spinach, thawed and squeezed dry
- 1 cup shredded mozzarella cheese
- ½ cup fresh shredded Parmesan cheese
- ½ teaspoon freshly ground black pepper, or to taste
- ¼ teaspoon salt, or to taste

1. Preheat your grill to 425°F for indirect cooking.

2. Remove the stems from the mushrooms and scrape out the gills on the undersides. Discard the gills.

3. Brush both sides of the mushrooms with 2 tablespoons of the oil and place them cap-side down on the grill for 5 minutes.

4. Finely chop the mushroom stems. In a large nonstick skillet, heat the remaining 1 teaspoon of the oil over medium heat. Add the onion, garlic, mushroom stems, and pepper and cook until the vegetables are tender, 5 to 7 minutes.

5. In a medium bowl, combine the cream cheese and sour cream and mix until fluffy. Fold in the cooked onion mixture, the spinach, ½ cup of the mozzarella cheese, and the Parmesan cheese. Season with the salt and pepper.

6. Remove the mushrooms from the grill, place on a wire baking rack, and fill with the spinach mixture. Top with the remaining ½ cup mozzarella cheese.

7. Grill on the indirect side for 12 to 16 minutes, until heated through and the cheese is browned.

8. Serve immediately.

CHEAT SHEET

Adding shredded chicken to the spinach mixture makes this vegetarian dish a carnivore's delight!

GRILLED CAULIFLOWER STEAK

SERVES 6

By no means will I ever try to convince anyone to take the word "steak" in the title literally, but this recipe is a unique way to prepare a vegetable that's often pureed or turned into "rice" into something a little more my speed. It's remarkably simple and straightforward: I keep the overall structure of the cauliflower intact, season it well, and slap it on a grill to add that chargrilled flavor and texture for a "steak" that even I can get behind.

2 large heads cauliflower

¼ cup extra virgin olive oil

Kosher salt and freshly cracked black pepper

2 teaspoons smoked paprika

1 teaspoon garlic powder

1. Preheat your grill to medium-high heat.

2. Remove the outer leaves from each cauliflower head. Cut off the bottom stems to create a flat base.

3. Use a large, sharp knife to trim away the sides, then cut the remaining head into 3 "steaks."

4. Brush the cauliflower steaks with the oil and sprinkle with salt, pepper, the smoked paprika, and the garlic powder.

5. Place the cauliflower steaks on the hot grill, cover, and cook for 6 minutes, or until the bottom begins to char. Flip the cauliflower, close the lid again, and grill for an additional 5 minutes, or until the cauliflower is tender.

6. Remove from the grill and enjoy immediately.

CHEAT SHEET

After you cut and trim the cauliflower steaks, you can save what's left over to create the previously mentioned cauliflower puree or "rice."

CORN RIBS

This is one of those recipes where the presentation completely changes the experience of the ingredient. By slicing the corn cobs into "ribs," you can transform traditional corn on the cob into little corn riblets that make for the perfect finger food. And just like our tomatoes, you won't find any better corn than in New Jersey. If you come visit someday, just hit me up—I got you!

4 ears fresh corn

2 tablespoons unsalted butter, melted

1 teaspoon smoked paprika

1 teaspoon garlic powder

1 teaspoon chili powder

1 teaspoon kosher salt

Lime wedges, for serving (optional)

1. Preheat your grill to medium-high heat.

2. Shuck the corn and remove the husks and silk. I like to microwave the corn for 2 minutes to soften it slightly, then let it cool. This enables it to grill faster without charring too much.

3. Place the corn on a cutting board, and, with a sharp chef's knife, cut both ends off the cobs to make a flat surface. I prefer the full corn ribs, but if you want to make it a little easier, you can cut the cobs in half crosswise. Stand each piece of corn up vertically on its flat end and cut it in half, cutting down the top of the corn cob through the center. Lay each half on the flat side, then cut in quarters.

4. Combine the melted butter, paprika, garlic powder, chili powder, and salt in a small bowl.

5. Pour most of the mixture onto the corn ribs (reserve some of the sauce for later). Toss to coat the corn with the sauce.

6. Grill the seasoned corn ribs kernel-side down for 6 to 8 minutes, until curled up and lightly charred. Flip and cook on the cut side for about 1 minute, then remove from the grill.

7. Add an extra brush of the leftover butter along with a squeeze of lime (if using) and serve.

CHEAT SHEET

I know we are spoiled for corn in Jersey, but do your best to choose fresh ears of corn with plump kernels and bright green husks for the best flavor and texture. Avoid corn with dried or shriveled kernels.

GRILLED EGGPLANT
WITH **FETA SALSA**

SERVES 6

Eggplant Parmesan is a vegetarian classic, but sometimes Kristin gets a little bored of it. This recipe is a fresh and vibrant alternative that's perfect for spring and summer. Eggplant holds up great on the grill—the more char the better! Between the tart balsamic glaze and the tangy feta salsa, this is a crowd-pleaser for carnivores and vegetarians alike.

For the Eggplant:

2 large eggplants, sliced into ½-inch-thick rounds

Extra virgin olive oil, for brushing

Kosher salt and freshly cracked black pepper

For the Feta Salsa:

¾ cup crumbled feta cheese

2 medium tomatoes, diced

½ cup diced red onion

½ cup chopped fresh basil

1 tablespoon fresh lemon juice

2 tablespoons extra virgin olive oil

Kosher salt and freshly cracked black pepper

2 tablespoons balsamic glaze

1. Preheat your grill to medium-high heat.

2. Brush both sides of the eggplant slices with oil and season with salt and pepper.

3. Place the eggplant slices on the grill and cook for 4 to 5 minutes per side, until tender and grill marks appear. Remove from the grill and set aside.

4. Make the salsa: In a medium bowl, combine the cheese, tomatoes, onion, basil, lemon juice, and oil. Mix well to combine and season with salt and pepper.

5. Arrange the grilled eggplant slices on a serving platter and top with a spoonful of the tomato feta salsa. Drizzle with the balsamic glaze and serve.

CHEAT SHEET

To remove excess moisture and bitterness from the eggplant, salt the slices and let them sit for 15 to 30 minutes before grilling. Pat the slices dry with a paper towel before grilling to remove the excess salt and moisture.

GRILLED GUACAMOLE

SERVES 4

Ever tried grilling your guacamole? If not, consider this your sign to get with the program! The trickiest part about this recipe is finding the ever-elusive, perfectly ripe avocado. After that, it's smooth sailing—just fire up the grill, gather the rest of your classic guac ingredients, and prepare to unlock a whole new dimension of smoky flavor.

1 large red onion, cut into rings

1 jalapeño chile, sliced in half and seeded

2 tomatoes, sliced in half

4 avocados, halved and pitted

1 tablespoon extra virgin olive oil

Juice of 2 to 3 limes

Kosher salt and freshly cracked black pepper

Handful of fresh cilantro leaves, chopped

Tortilla chips, for serving

1. Preheat your grill to medium-high heat.

2. Combine the onion rings, jalapeño, tomatoes, and avocados in a large bowl and toss with the oil.

3. Place everything on the grill cut-side down and grill until charred.

4. Remove from grill and cool. Chop the onions and place them in a bowl. Add the lime juice, season with salt and pepper, and toss to coat.

5. Let the onions sit for a few minutes. Chop the jalapeño and tomato and add to the bowl with the onions. Add the grilled avocado and mash to your desired texture.

6. Stir in the cilantro, taste, and season with salt and pepper as needed.

7. Serve with tortilla chips.

SWEET AND SPICY GRILLED SWEET POTATO WEDGES

SERVES 8

My sons, Aidric and Nash, are picky about texture—anything mashed or blended is pretty hit or miss. So, after they rejected a mashed sweet potato recipe, I went back to the drawing board and came up with this. Since my boys can handle a little spice, I aimed for a perfect balance of sweet and spicy with these grilled sweet potato wedges. They're easy to make and great if you're looking for a sweet potato recipe with a spicy kick.

4 medium sweet potatoes

3 tablespoons extra virgin olive oil

2 tablespoons honey

1 teaspoon smoked paprika

½ teaspoon cayenne pepper

Kosher salt and freshly cracked black pepper

1. Preheat your grill to medium-high heat.

2. Cut the sweet potatoes in half lengthwise. Place each half cut-side down on the cutting board and cut each half lengthwise again. This will give you 4 large wedges. Cut each wedge in half lengthwise for 8 wedges per sweet potato.

3. In a large bowl, whisk the oil, honey, smoked paprika, and cayenne and season with salt and pepper.

4. Toss the sweet potato wedges in the mixture.

5. Grill for about 15 minutes, flipping every few minutes, until caramelized, cooked through, and fork-tender. I like to keep a toothpick handy to test.

6. Serve immediately.

SOY AND GINGER-MARINATED GRILLED TOFU

SERVES 4

The beautiful thing about tofu is that it does an incredible job of taking on whatever flavors you want to create! Given that my wife is vegetarian, I have thrown down a fair amount of tofu on the grill. This is my go-to recipe when she's in the mood for an Asian-inspired meal that's quick and simple. Happy wife, happy life!

1 block extra-firm tofu

Kosher salt and freshly cracked black pepper

¼ cup soy sauce

2 tablespoons sesame oil

Juice of 1 lime

2 tablespoons light brown sugar

1 tablespoon grated ginger

2 cloves garlic, minced

Sliced green onions, for garnish

1. Preheat your grill to medium-high heat.

2. Put the tofu slices on a paper towel–lined baking sheet and top with more paper towels. Press gently to remove the moisture. Remove the paper towels, cut into ½-inch-thick slices, and season with salt and pepper on both sides.

3. Whisk the soy sauce, oil, lime juice, brown sugar, ginger, and garlic in a medium bowl.

4. Put the tofu in a zip-top bag. Pour half the marinade over the tofu to coat. Save the remaining marinade to brush while grilling and/or for serving.

5. Place the tofu on the grill at an angle across the grates (for grill marks, if you care about that kind of thing). Grill for 4 to 5 minutes, flip, and repeat on the other side.

6. Remove from the grill and brush with some of the remaining marinade. Garnish with green onions and serve.

FIRE-ROASTED BRUSCHETTA

SERVES 4

Hand me a menu at any Italian restaurant and you'd better believe bruschetta is the first thing I'm ordering. It's easily one of my wife's favorite starters as well. Thankfully, it's an even more delicious dish to make in the comfort of your own backyard. Just get those tomatoes sizzling on the grill and let that chargrilled flavor work its magic. And sorry to brag again, but there is just no match for Jersey tomatoes!

1 clove garlic, finely chopped

¼ cup balsamic vinegar

1 teaspoon brown sugar

4 Roma tomatoes, sliced ½ inch thick

Extra virgin olive oil, for brushing

Kosher salt and freshly cracked black pepper

1 baguette

1 bunch green onions

2 cloves garlic

4 tablespoons basil, sliced into ribbons

1. Preheat your grill to medium-high heat.

2. In a small bowl, combine the 1 clove finely chopped garlic, the vinegar, and the brown sugar and mix until the sugar dissolves and is completely combined.

3. Brush the sliced tomatoes with oil and season well with salt and pepper. Place the tomatoes on the grill over direct heat and brush the tops with the vinegar mixture.

4. Grill the tomatoes for 3 to 4 minutes, then flip and brush with more of the vinegar mixture. Grill for another 3 to 4 minutes.

5. While the tomatoes are grilling, slice the baguette and brush the slices with oil. Place on the grill until crispy and charred.

6. Remove the baguette slices from the grill and give them 5 minutes to cool.

7. Peel the skin off the tomatoes—it will come off easily. Coarsely chop the tomatoes and place them in a medium bowl.

8. Stir in the green onions, 2 cloves garlic, and basil. Season with salt and pepper.

9. Place a healthy tablespoon of the tomato mixture on top of the grilled baguette slices, add a little pinch of salt, and serve.

CHEAT SHEET

- For the best flavor, opt for ripe, juicy tomatoes. Roma tomatoes are commonly used for bruschetta because of their firm texture and low moisture content, but you can use any variety you like.

- For an extra bite of flavor, shave some Parmesan cheese on top of the bruschetta.

SMOKED SPINACH AND ARTICHOKE DIP

SERVES 8

Spinach and artichoke dip is another classic vegetarian favorite that is due for a smoky twist. This super-simple recipe brings together all the goodness of cheese and spinach and the tanginess of artichokes and infuses it all with a slight hint of smoke. The result is a dip that's an absolute hit with everyone.

1 round loaf pumpernickel bread

Extra virgin olive oil, for drizzling

Garlic salt

10 ounces frozen chopped spinach, defrosted

8 ounces cream cheese, softened

1 cup sour cream

½ cup mayonnaise

2 cloves garlic

One 14-ounce jar marinated artichokes, drained and chopped

½ cup freshly shredded Parmesan cheese

1½ cups shredded mozzarella cheese

1. Preheat the oven to 350°F.

2. Cut the top off the pumpernickel loaf and remove the center, leaving a ¾-inch shell.

3. Cut the top and insides of the loaf into bite-sized squares for dipping. Drizzle with oil and sprinkle with garlic salt. Bake for 5 minutes.

4. Squeeze as much liquid out of the spinach as you can. Set aside.

5. Beat the cream cheese, sour cream, and mayonnaise with a mixer on medium speed until fluffy.

6. Using a spoon, stir in the garlic, spinach, artichokes, Parmesan cheese, and 1 cup of the mozzarella cheese. Microwave for 5 minutes, stirring after 3 minutes.

7. Place the cheese mixture into the bread bowl. Top with the remaining ½ cup mozzarella cheese.

8. Bake uncovered for 25 to 30 minutes, until the cheese is melted and the center is hot.

9. Remove from oven, let cool, and serve.

COFFEE-RUBBED SMOKED CREAM CHEESE

SERVES 4 TO 6

I was not a big believer in smoked cream cheese when the recipe made its rounds across social media. I love cream cheese, but I just wasn't convinced that smoking would elevate it to a next-level type of dish. With this recipe, I admit defeat and will tell you this is worth the extraordinarily little bit of time and effort involved. I also went ahead and doubled down on the breakfast theme by adding my coffee dry rub for a kick of caffeine. It's not a groundbreaking idea, but the smoke and seasoning pair perfectly—trust me, give it a try!

One (8-ounce) block cream cheese

1 tablespoon Sweet and Spicy Pork Rub (page 150)

1 tablespoon Coffee Dry Rub (page 151)

1. Preheat your smoker to 180°F. Fruitwood works best for this recipe (I use applewood). You're smoking at a low temperature to infuse plenty of smoke without melting the cream cheese. Line a baking sheet with aluminum foil.

2. Score the block of cream cheese in a crosshatch pattern.

3. Combine the two rubs in a small bowl and season the entire block of cream cheese with the rub mixture.

4. Place the block of cream cheese on the prepared baking sheet, put it in the smoker, and smoke for 2 hours.

5. Remove from the smoker and let cool for a few minutes.

6. My favorite way to serve this is with pepper jelly and Ritz crackers, but you can use pita or any other sturdy cracker you like.

ACKNOWLEDGMENTS

First and foremost, I want to express my love and gratitude to my beautiful wife. Kristin, these pages would have never been possible without your love, support, knowledge, expertise, and, most of all, patience! Your footprint can be found on every page of this book. You brought these recipes to life with your photography. I love you!

Aidric and Nash, my boys! The inspiration behind Groark Boys BBQ and my culinary partners in crime. You are the best taste testers a cook could ask for! You bring so much joy and laughter into our home and you challenge me to be the best dad I can be.

Kurt Halls: an Instagram direct message that became the beginning of a journey. You were the first person in this crazy world of social media who saw something and encouraged me to lead with my heart, build real relationships, and go all in. You are a mentor and, more important, a friend. Thank you!

If you are reading this and ever viewed, liked, shared, or supported any of my videos or charitable causes, THANK YOU! I have been able to turn a passion into a career filled with amazing opportunities thanks to the love and support of so many people. Some I have met, some I have yet to meet. The questions, words of encouragement, and constructive and not-so-constructive criticism motivate and push me to get to the "Next Level," and for that I feel forever blessed!

INDEX

Page numbers of recipe photos appear in italics.

achiote paste

Al Pastor–Style Marinade, 47

Alabama White BBQ Sauce, 144, *145*

All-Purpose BBQ Rub, 150

almonds

Crunchy Broccoli Salad, *168*, 168–69

Al Pastor–Style Pulled Pork, *46*, 46–47

American cheese

Bacon, Egg, and Cheese with Homemade English Muffins, *202*, 202–4

apple juice

Al Pastor–Style Marinade, 47

Groark Boys Pulled Pork, *20*, 28–30

apples

Prosciutto-Wrapped Brie, *216*, 216–17

Smoked Apple Crisp, *190*, 191

Applewood Smoked Beer Can Chicken, *84*, 85

artichokes, jarred

Smoked Spinach and Artichoke Dip, 240, *241*

avocados

Grilled Fish Tacos with Chipotle Lime Dressing, *118*, 118–19

Grilled Guacamole, 232, *233*

Backyard Jersey Cheesesteak, *206*, 206–7

bacon

Bacon, Egg, and Cheese with Homemade English Muffins, *202*, 202–4

Candied Bacon, *181*, 182

Next-Level Bone-In Veal Chops with Bacon and Bell Pepper Ragu, *134*, 134–36

Smoked Bacon Beans, *162*, 162–63

Smoked Bacon-Wrapped Scallops, *200*, 200–201

Smoked BBQ Bacon-Wrapped Drumsticks, *98*, 98–99

Smoked Pig Shots, 208, *209*

bananas

Banana Pudding, *186*, 186–87

BBQ Banana Split, *188*, 188–89

how to grill, 189

basil

Feta Salsa, *230*, 230–31

Fire-Roasted Bruschetta, *238*, 238–39

Lemon and Herb Marinated Chicken Thighs, *86*, 86–87

Basting Liquid, 45

BBQ Banana Split, *188*, 188–89

BBQ Peach-Glazed Chicken Kabobs, 90, *91*

BBQ sauces
  Alabama White, 144, *145*
  Classic Sweet BBQ Sauce, *145*, 147
  Mustard-Based BBQ Sauce, 144, *145*
  Vinegar-Based Carolina BBQ Sauce, *145*, 146

BBQ tips, 20, 22

beans
  Smoked Bacon Beans, *162*, 162–63
  beef, 20, 51
  Backyard Jersey Cheesesteak, *206*, 206–7
  Beef Tallow Campfire Fries, *220*, 220–21
  Cheddar and Mozzarella–Stuffed Smoked Burgers, *60*, 60–61
  Chuck Roast Burnt Ends, 66–67, *67*
  Grilled Steak Fajitas, *52*, 52–53
  Kalbi-Style Korean BBQ Short Ribs, 64, *65*
  Next-Level Filet Mignon Sandwich with Gorgonzola Crema and Blueberry Sauce, 54–55, *55*
  Perfectly Smoked Backyard Brisket, *74*, 74–76
  Reverse-Seared Bone-in Ribeye Steak, *68*, 68–69
  Smoked Beef Short Ribs, *70*, 71–73
  Smoked Dino Ribs, *50*, 57–58, *59*
  Smoked Tri-Tip with Chimichurri Sauce, *62*, 62–63
  temperature chart, 20
  what plate ribs are, 57
  what tri-tip is, 62

beer
  Applewood Smoked Beer Can Chicken, *84*, 85
  berries
  Smoked Berry Cobbler, *184*, 184–85

Big T's Smoked Mac and Cheese, *158*, 158–60

Blackened Cajun Seasoning, 152

black pepper
  All-Purpose BBQ Rub, 150
  Blackened Cajun Seasoning, 152
  Coffee Dry Rub, 151
  Memphis-Style Rib Rub, 152
  Poultry Rub, 151
  Sweet and Spicy Pork Rub, 150

Blueberry Sauce, 54–55, *55*

blue cheese
  Elk Burgers with Caramelized Onions and Blue Cheese, *138*, 138–39

branzino
  Smoked Lemon Herb Whole Branzino, *108*, 108–9

brie
  Prosciutto-Wrapped Brie, *216*, 216–17

"Brisket" Style Pork Belly, 48, *49*

broccoli
  Crunchy Broccoli Salad, *168*, 168–69

brown sugar
  All-Purpose BBQ Rub, 150
  Classic Sweet BBQ Sauce, *145*, 147

Coffee Dry Rub, 151

Hot Buttered Rum, 195–96

Memphis-Style Rib Rub, 152

Pickle Glaze, 147

Sweet and Spicy Pork Rub, 150

Vinegar-Based Carolina BBQ Sauce, 146

Bruschetta, Fire-Roasted, *238*, 238–39

burgers

Cast-Iron Salmon Burgers, *110*, 110–11

Cheddar and Mozzarella–Stuffed Smoked
Burgers, *60*, 60–61

Elk Burgers with Caramelized Onions and
Blue Cheese, *138*, 138–39

Goat Cheese–Stuffed Veal Burgers, *132*,
132–33

butter

Garlic Butter, 107

Herb Butter, 140

Honey Butter Cream, 180–82, *181*

Hot Buttered Rum, 195–96

cabbage

Grilled Fish Tacos with Chipotle Lime
Dressing, *118*, 118–19

Smack Slaw, *156*, 156–57

cake

Chocolate Dump Cake, *192*, 192–93

Sopapilla (cheesecake), *194*, 194–96

Campfire S'mores Dip, *212*, 212–13

Candied Bacon, *181*, 182

Caramelized Onions, *138*, 139

carrot

Smack Slaw, *156*, 156–57

Cast-Iron Salmon Burgers, *110*, 110–11

Cast-Iron Shrimp Scampi, 112, *113*

cauliflower

Grilled Cauliflower Steak, 226, *227*

cayenne pepper

All-Purpose BBQ Rub, 150

Blackened Cajun Seasoning, 152

Coffee Dry Rub, 151

Memphis-Style Rib Rub, 152

Sweet and Spicy Grilled Sweet Potato
Wedges, *234*, 235

Sweet and Spicy Pork Rub, 150

Cedar Plank Salmon, *116*, 116–17

cheddar cheese

Big T's Smoked Mac and Cheese, *158*,
158–60

Cheddar and Mozzarella–Stuffed Smoked
Burgers, *60*, 60–61

Jalapeno Corn Bread, *166*, 166–67

Smoked Buffalo Chicken Dip, *218*, 219

Smoked Pig Shots, 208, *209*

cherries

Chocolate Dump Cake, *192*, 192–93

chicken, 79

Applewood Smoked Beer Can Chicken,
84, 85

BBQ Peach-Glazed Chicken Kabobs, 90,
91

Grilled Romaine Chicken Caesar Salad, *82*, 82–83

Honey-Mustard Glazed Wings, 96, *97*

how to spatchcock, 81

Jerk Marinated Chicken Thighs, *92*, 92–94

Lemon and Herb Marinated Chicken Thighs, *86*, 86–87

Poultry Rub, 151

refrigerating or freezing leftovers, 87

resting a whole chicken, 22

Smoked BBQ Bacon-Wrapped Drumsticks, *98*, 98–99

Smoked BBQ Spatchcock Chicken, *80*, 80–81

Smoked Buffalo Chicken Dip, *218*, 219

Smoked Pickle-Glazed Chicken Wings, *88*, 89

temperature chart, 20

temperature recommendation, 94

chili powder

All-Purpose BBQ Rub, 150

Al Pastor–Style Marinade, 47

Coffee Dry Rub, 151

Memphis-Style Rib Rub, 152

Sweet and Spicy Pork Rub, 150

Chimichurri, *62*, 63

Chimichurri, Mint, 127

Chipotle Lime Dressing, 119

chives

Herb Butter, 140

chocolate

Campfire S'mores Dip, *212*, 212–13

Chocolate Dump Cake, *192*, 192–93

Chuck Roast Burnt Ends, 66–67, *67*

cilantro

Chimichurri, *62*, 63

Grilled Fish Tacos with Chipotle Lime Dressing, *118*, 118–19

Grilled Guacamole, 232, *233*

Classic Sweet BBQ Sauce, *145*, 147

Cobbler, Smoked Berry, *184*, 184–85

coffee

Coffee Dry Rub, 151

Coffee-Rubbed Smoked Cream Cheese, *242*, 243

Collard Greens, *164*, 165

Cooper Sharp American cheese

Backyard Jersey Cheesesteak, *206*, 206–7

corn

Corn Ribs, *228*, 228–29

Grilled Mexican Street Corn, *176*, 177

Mom-Mom Betty's Corn Pudding, *172*, 173

cornmeal

Corn Bread Cupcakes with Honey Butter Cream and Candied Bacon, 180–82, *181*

Jalapeno Corn Bread, *166*, 166–67

cotija cheese

Grilled Mexican Street Corn, *176*, 177

cranberries

    Crunchy Broccoli Salad, *168*, 168–69

cream cheese

    Coffee-Rubbed Smoked Cream Cheese, *242*, 243

    Smoked Buffalo Chicken Dip, *218*, 219

    Smoked Pig Shots, 208, *209*

    Smoked Spinach and Artichoke Dip, 240, *241*

    Sopapilla (cheesecake), *194*, 194–96

    Stuffed Portobello Mushrooms, *224*, 224 25

Creamy Dill Dipping Sauce, *104*, 104–5

Crisp, Smoked Apple, *190*, 191

Crunchy Broccoli Salad, *168*, 168–69

cucumber

    Tzatziki, 131, *131*

cumin

    Al Pastor–Style Marinade, 47

    Memphis-Style Rib Rub, 152

    Sweet and Spicy Pork Rub, 150

Cupcakes, Corn Bread, 180–82, *181*

dill

    Creamy Dill Dipping Sauce, *104*, 104–5

    marinade for salmon, 117

    Tzatziki, 131, *131*

dips

    Creamy Dill Dipping Sauce, *104*, 104–5

    Smoked Buffalo Chicken Dip, *218*, 219

Smoked Spinach and Artichoke Dip, 240, *241*

Donna's Pineapple Bake, 174, *175*

Dry-Rubbed Pork Tenderloin, *42*, 42–43

eggplant

    Grilled Eggplant with Feta Salsa, *230*, 230–31

    eggs

    Bacon, Egg, and Cheese with Homemade English Muffins, *202*, 202–4

    Donna's Pineapple Bake, 174, *175*

elk

    Elk Burgers with Caramelized Onions and Blue Cheese, *138*, 138–39

    Grilled Elk Tenderloin with Herb Butter, 140–41, *141*

English Muffins, *202*, 202–4

Fajitas, Grilled Steak, *52*, 52–53

feta cheese

    Feta Salsa, *230*, 230–31

    Grilled Mexican Street Corn, *176*, 177

Fire-Roasted Bruschetta, *238*, 238–39

garlic

    Garlic Butter, 107

    Grilled Garlic-Lime Shrimp Skewers with Vegetables, *120*, 121

    Grilled Lemon Garlic Scallops, *114*, 115

Herb Butter, 140

lemon-herb marinade for chicken, 87

marinade for salmon, 117

Smoked Leg of Lamb with Garlic and
Rosemary, *124*, 125

garlic powder

All-Purpose BBQ Rub, 150

Blackened Cajun Seasoning, 152

Coffee Dry Rub, 151

Memphis-Style Rib Rub, 152

Poultry Rub, 151

Sweet and Spicy Pork Rub, 150

ginger

Pineapple-Ginger Glaze, 32–33

Soy and Ginger Marinated Grilled Tofu,
236, *237*

glazes

Maple Dijon Glaze, 35–36

Peach Glaze, 90

Pickle Glaze, 147

Pineapple-Ginger Glaze, 32–33

Goat Cheese–Stuffed Veal Burgers, *132*, 132–33

Gorgonzola Crema, 54–55, *55*

graham crackers

Campfire S'mores Dip, *212*, 212–13

green onions

Fire-Roasted Bruschetta, *238*, 238–39

Grilled Cauliflower Steak, 226, *227*

Grilled Eggplant with Feta Salsa, *230*, 230–31

Grilled Elk Tenderloin with Herb Butter, 140–41,
141

Grilled Fish Tacos with Chipotle Lime Dressing,
118, 118–19

Grilled Guacamole, 232, *233*

Grilled Lamb Loin Chops, *128*, 129

Grilled Lemon Garlic Scallops, *114*, 115

Grilled Mexican Street Corn, *176*, 177

Grilled Peaches, *194*, 194–96

Grilled Pork Chops with Pineapple-Ginger Glaze,
32, 32–33

Grilled Romaine Chicken Caesar Salad, *82*,
82–83

Grilled Sausage and Pepper Sammy, *214*, 215

Grilled Steak Fajitas, *52*, 52–53

grilling

adding a smoky flavor, 129, 139

BBQ tips, 20, 22

grill heat temperature settings, 22

indirect or direct, two-zone cooking, 15,
22

insulated hot box for resting meat, such as
Cambro GoBox, 30

meat temperature chart, 20

resting meat, 22

reverse sear method, 68–69

safety supplies/equipment, 17, 20

supply list, 16–17

using a kettle-style grill as a smoker, 39

vocabulary, 15–16

Groark Boys Pulled Pork, *20*, 28–30

Guacamole, Grilled, 232, *233*

halibut
    Grilled Fish Tacos with Chipotle Lime
        Dressing, *118*, 118–19

Hasselback Potatoes, *170*, 170–71

honey
    Honey Butter Cream, 180–82, *181*
    Honey-Mustard Glazed Wings, 96, *97*
    Mustard-Based BBQ Sauce, 144, *145*
    Pickle Glaze, 147
    salmon marinade, 117
    Sweet and Spicy Grilled Sweet Potato
        Wedges, *234*, 235

horseradish
    Alabama White BBQ Sauce, 144, *145*

Hot Buttered Rum, 195–96

hot sauce
    Smoked Buffalo Chicken Dip, *218*, 219
    Vinegar-Based Carolina BBQ Sauce, 146

ice cream
    BBQ Banana Split, *188*, 188–89
    Smoked Apple Crisp, *190*, 191
    Smoked Berry Cobbler, *184*, 184–85

jalapeño chiles
    Jalapeno Corn Bread, *166*, 166–67
    Smoked Pig Shots, 208, *209*

Jerk Marinated Chicken Thighs, *92*, 92–94

Jerk Seasoning, 93

Jerk Wet Rub, 93–94

kabobs and skewers
    BBQ Peach-Glazed Chicken Kabobs, 90,
        91
    Grilled Garlic-Lime Shrimp Skewers with
        Vegetables, *120*, 121
    Lamb Kabobs with Tzatziki, 130–31, *131*
    Shrimp and Sausage Skewers, *210*, 211

Kalbi-Style Korean BBQ Short Ribs, 64, 65

ketchup
    Classic Sweet BBQ Sauce, *145*, 147
    Mustard-Based BBQ Sauce, 144, *145*
    Vinegar-Based Carolina BBQ Sauce, 146

lamb
    Grilled Lamb Loin Chops, *128*, 129
    Lamb Kabobs with Tzatziki, 130–31, *131*
    Smoked and Grilled Rack of Lamb, *126*,
        126–27
    Smoked Leg of Lamb with Garlic and
        Rosemary, *124*, 125

lemon
    Alabama White BBQ Sauce, 144, *145*
    Grilled Lemon Garlic Scallops, *114*, 115

Lemon and Herb Marinated Chicken Thighs, *86*, 86–87

marinade for salmon, 117

Smoked Lemon Herb Whole Branzino, *108*, 108–9

lime

Chipotle Lime Dressing, 119

Grilled Garlic-Lime Shrimp Skewers with Vegetables, *120*, 121

lobster

Smoked Garlic Butter Lobster Tails, *106*, 106–7

Mac and Cheese, Big T's Smoked, *158*, 158–60

maple syrup

Maple Dijon Glaze, 35–36

marinades

Al Pastor–Style, 47

for chicken, 86–87

for Korean short ribs, 64

for salmon, 117

marshmallows

Campfire S'mores Dip, *212*, 212–13

mayonnaise

Alabama White BBQ Sauce, 144, *145*

Caesar Salad, *82*, 82–83

Chipotle Lime Dressing, 119

Smoked Spinach and Artichoke Dip, 240, *241*

Memphis-Style Rib Rub, 152

Mint Chimichurri, 127

molasses

Classic Sweet BBQ Sauce, *145*, 147

Mom-Mom Betty's Corn Pudding, *172*, 173

mozzarella cheese

Big T's Smoked Mac and Cheese, *158*, 158–60

Cheddar and Mozzarella–Stuffed Smoked Burgers, *60*, 60–61

Smoked Spinach and Artichoke Dip, 240, *241*

Stuffed Portobello Mushrooms, *224*, 224–25

Muffins, English, *202*, 202–4

mushrooms

BBQ Peach-Glazed Chicken Kabobs, 90, *91*

Stuffed Portobello Mushrooms, *224*, 224–25

mustard

Honey-Mustard Glazed Wings, 96, *97*

Maple Dijon Glaze, 35–36

Memphis-Style Rib Rub, 152

Mustard-Based BBQ Sauce, 144, *145*

Pickle Glaze, 147

used as a binder, 39

Next-Level Bone-In Veal Chops with Bacon and Bell Pepper Ragu, *134*, 134–36

Next-Level Filet Mignon Sandwich with Gorgonzola Crema and Blueberry Sauce, 54–55, *55*

olive oil
>Chimichurri, 63

>Jerk Wet Rub, 94

>lemon-herb marinade for chicken, 87

>marinade for salmon, 117

>Mint Chimichurri, 127

onion powder
>All-Purpose BBQ Rub, 150

>Blackened Cajun Seasoning, 152

>Coffee Dry Rub, 151

>Memphis-Style Rib Rub, 152

>Poultry Rub, 151

>Sweet and Spicy Pork Rub, 150

onions
>Backyard Jersey Cheesesteak, *206*, 206–7

>BBQ Peach-Glazed Chicken Kabobs, 90, *91*

>Elk Burgers with Caramelized Onions and Blue Cheese, *138*, 138–39

>Feta Salsa, *230*, 230–31

>Grilled Garlic-Lime Shrimp Skewers with Vegetables, *120*, 121

>Grilled Guacamole, 232, *233*

>Grilled Sausage and Pepper Sammy, *214*, 215

>Grilled Steak Fajitas, *52*, 52–53

>Lamb Kabobs with Tzatziki, 130–31, *131*

>Smack Slaw, *156*, 156–57

oregano
>Blackened Cajun Seasoning, 152

>Poultry Rub, 151

paprika
>All-Purpose BBQ Rub, 150

>Blackened Cajun Seasoning, 152

>Coffee Dry Rub, 151

>Memphis-Style Rib Rub, 152

>Sweet and Spicy Grilled Sweet Potato Wedges, *234*, 235

>Sweet and Spicy Pork Rub, 150

Parmesan cheese
>Big T's Smoked Mac and Cheese, *158*, 158–60

>Smoked Spinach and Artichoke Dip, 240, *241*

>Stuffed Portobello Mushrooms, *224*, 224–25

parsley
>Chimichurri, *62*, 63

>Mint Chimichurri, 127

>Poultry Rub, 151

pasta
>Big T's Smoked Mac and Cheese, *158*, 158–60

peaches
>Grilled Peaches, *194*, 194–96

>Peach Glaze, 90

peppers, bell
>BBQ Peach-Glazed Chicken Kabobs, 90, *91*

>Grilled Garlic-Lime Shrimp Skewers with Vegetables, *120*, 121

>Grilled Sausage and Pepper Sammy, *214*, 215

>Grilled Steak Fajitas, *52*, 52–53

Lamb Kabobs with Tzatziki, 130–31, *131*

Bone-In Veal Chops with Bacon and Bell Pepper Ragu, *134*, 134–36

Perfectly Smoked Backyard Brisket, *74*, 74–76

pickle juice
 as a brine for chicken, 89
 Pickle Glaze, 147

pineapple
 Al Pastor–Style Marinade, 47
 Donna's Pineapple Bake, 174, *175*
 Pineapple-Ginger Glaze, 32–33

pork, 27
 Al Pastor–Style Pulled Pork, *46*, 46–47
 "Brisket" Style Pork Belly, 48, *49*
 cuts of, 27, 28
 Dry-Rubbed Pork Tenderloin, *42*, 42–43
 Grilled Pork Chops with Pineapple-Ginger Glaze, *32*, 32–33
 Grilled Pork Steaks, *44*, 44–45
 Groark Boys Pulled Pork, 28–30, *29*
 Pork Belly Burnt Ends, 40, *41*
 refrigeration for cooked dishes, 31
 resting meat, 33
 scoring meat, 31
 searing meat, 36
 Smoked Pickle-Glazed Baby Back Pork Ribs, 36–38, *37*
 Stuffed Pork Loin with Maple Dijon Glaze, *34*, 35–36
 Sweet and Spicy Pork Rub, 150
 temperature chart for, 20

potatoes
 Beef Tallow Campfire Fries, *220*, 220–21
 Hasselback Potatoes, *170*, 170–71

Poultry Rub, 151

Prosciutto-Wrapped Brie, *216*, 216–17

provolone cheese
 Backyard Jersey Cheesesteak, *206*, 206–7

pudding
 Banana Pudding, *186*, 186–87
 Mom-Mom Betty's Corn Pudding, *172*, 173

pulled pork
 Al Pastor–Style Pulled Pork, *46*, 46–47
 cheat sheet for, 31
 Groark Boys Pulled Pork, 28–30, *29*

Reverse-Seared Bone-in Ribeye Steak, *68*, 68–69

ribs
 Kalbi-Style Korean BBQ Short Ribs, 64, *65*
 Memphis-Style Rib Rub, 152
 Smoked Beef Short Ribs, *70*, 71–73
 Smoked Dino Ribs, *50*, 57–58, *59*
 Smoked Pickle-Glazed Baby Back Pork Ribs, 36–38, *37*
 smoking cheat sheet, 73

romaine lettuce
 Caesar Salad, *82*, 82–83
 how to grill, 83

rosemary

 Herb Butter, 140

 Lemon and Herb Marinated Chicken
  Thighs, *86*, 86–87

 Poultry Rub, 151

 Smoked Leg of Lamb with Garlic and
  Rosemary, *124*, 125

 Smoked Lemon Herb Whole Branzino,
  108, 108–9

rubs and seasonings, 147

 All-Purpose BBQ Rub, 150

 Blackened Cajun Seasoning, 152

 Coffee Dry Rub, 151

 Jerk Wet Rub, 93–94

 Memphis-Style Rib Rub, 152

 Poultry Rub, 151

 spice rub for pork tenderloin, 43

 Sweet and Spicy Pork Rub, 150

rum

 Hot Buttered Rum, 195–96

sage

 Poultry Rub, 151

salads

 Crunchy Broccoli Salad, *168*, 168–69

 Grilled Romaine Chicken Caesar Salad,
  82, 82–83

 Smack Slaw, *156*, 156–57

salmon

 Cast-Iron Salmon Burgers, *110*, 110–11

 Cedar Plank Salmon, *116*, 116–17

 Smoked Salmon Bites with Dill Dipping

  Sauce, *104*, 104–5

Salsa, Feta, *230*, 230–31

salt, kosher

 All-Purpose BBQ Rub, 150

 Blackened Cajun Seasoning, 152

 Coffee Dry Rub, 151

 Memphis-Style Rib Rub, 152

 Poultry Rub, 151

 Sweet and Spicy Pork Rub, 150

sandwiches

 Backyard Jersey Cheesesteak, *206*, 206–7

 Grilled Sausage and Pepper Sammy, *214*,
  215

 Next-level Filet Mignon Sandwich with
  Gorgonzola Crema and Blueberry
  Sauce, 54–55, *55*

sauces

 Alabama White BBQ Sauce, 144, *145*

 Blueberry Sauce, 54–55

 Chimichurri, *62*, 63

 Chipotle Lime Dressing, 119

 Classic Sweet BBQ Sauce, *145*, 147

 Creamy Dill Dipping Sauce, *104*, 104–5

 Hot Buttered Rum, 195–96

 Mustard-Based BBQ Sauce, 144, *145*

 Vinegar-Based Carolina BBQ Sauce, *145*,
  146

sausage

 Grilled Sausage and Pepper Sammy, *214*,
  215

 Shrimp and Sausage Skewers, *210*, 211

 Smoked Pig Shots, 208, *209*

scallops
    Grilled Lemon Garlic Scallops, *114*, 115
    Smoked Bacon-Wrapped Scallops, *200*, 200–201

seafood, 103
    Cast-Iron Salmon Burgers, *110*, 110–11
    Cast-Iron Shrimp Scampi, 112, *113*
    Cedar Plank Salmon, *116*, 116–17
    Grilled Fish Tacos with Chipotle Lime Dressing, *118*, 118–19
    Grilled Garlic-Lime Shrimp Skewers with Vegetables, *120*, 121
    Grilled Lemon Garlic Scallops, *114*, 115
    Shrimp and Sausage Skewers, *210*, 211
    Smoked Bacon-Wrapped Scallops, *200*, 200–201
    Smoked Garlic Butter Lobster Tails, *106*, 106–7
    Smoked Lemon Herb Whole Branzino, *108*, 108–9
    Smoked Salmon Bites with Dill Dipping Sauce, *104*, 104–5

shrimp
    Cast-Iron Shrimp Scampi, 112, *113*
    Grilled Garlic-Lime Shrimp Skewers with Vegetables, *120*, 121
    Shrimp and Sausage Skewers, *210*, 211

Smack Slaw, *156*, 156–57

Smoked and Grilled Rack of Lamb, *126*, 126–27

Smoked Apple Crisp, *190*, 191

Smoked Bacon Beans, *162*, 162–63

Smoked Bacon-Wrapped Scallops, *200*, 200–201

Smoked BBQ Bacon-Wrapped Drumsticks, *98*, 98–99

Smoked BBQ Spatchcock Chicken, *80*, 80–81

Smoked Beef Short Ribs, *70*, 71–73

Smoked Berry Cobbler, *184*, 184–85

Smoked Buffalo Chicken Dip, *218*, 219

Smoked Dino Ribs, *50*, 57–58, *59*

Smoked Garlic Butter Lobster Tails, *106*, 106–7

Smoked Leg of Lamb with Garlic and Rosemary, *124*, 125

Smoked Lemon Herb Whole Branzino, *108*, 108–9

Smoked Pickle-Glazed Baby Back Pork Ribs, 36–38, *37*

Smoked Pickle-Glazed Chicken Wings, *88*, 89

Smoked Pig Shots, 208, *209*

Smoked Salmon Bites with Dill Dipping Sauce, *104*, 104–5

Smoked Spinach and Artichoke Dip, 240, *241*

Smoked Tri-Tip with Chimichurri Sauce, *62*, 62–63

smokers/smoking food, 16
    adding smokey flavor, 22, 39
    "biscuit test" and identifying hot spots, 20, 22

fruit wood choices for smoking lamb, 127

spritzing with water or apple juice, 72

tips for smoking short ribs, 72

using a kettle-style grill as a smoker, 39

using applewood for pork, 37

using hickory for beef, 67, 75

using oakwood for beef, 63, 67, 71, 75

S'mores Dip, Campfire, *212*, 212–13

Sopapilla with Grilled Peaches and Hot Buttered Rum, *194*, 194–96

sour cream

Caesar Salad, *82*, 82–83

Smoked Spinach and Artichoke Dip, 240, *241*

Soy and Ginger Marinated Grilled Tofu, 236, *237*

Spice Rub, 43

spinach

Smoked Spinach and Artichoke Dip, 240, *241*

Stuffed Portobello Mushrooms, *224*, 224–25

steak

Grilled Steak Fajitas, *52*, 52–53

resting steaks, 22

Reverse-Seared Bone-in Ribeye Steak, *68*, 68–69

reverse sear method, 68–69

Stuffed Pork Loin with Maple Dijon Glaze, *34*, 35–36

Stuffed Portobello Mushrooms, *224*, 224–25

Sweet and Spicy Grilled Sweet Potato Wedges, *234*, 235

Sweet and Spicy Pork Rub, 150

sweet potatoes

Sweet and Spicy Grilled Sweet Potato Wedges, *234*, 235

tacos

Al Pastor–Style Pulled Pork, *46*, 46–47

Grilled Fish Tacos with Chipotle Lime Dressing, *118*, 118–19

temperature chart (meat), 20

thyme

Blackened Cajun Seasoning, 152

Herb Butter, 140

Lemon and Herb Marinated Chicken Thighs, *86*, 86–87

Poultry Rub, 151

Smoked Lemon Herb Whole Branzino, *108*, 108–9

tilapia

Grilled Fish Tacos with Chipotle Lime Dressing, *118*, 118–19

tofu

Soy and Ginger Marinated Grilled Tofu, 236, *237*

tomatoes

Feta Salsa, *230*, 230–31

Fire-Roasted Bruschetta, *238*, 238–39

Grilled Guacamole, 232, *233*

tomatoes, cherry

    BBQ Peach-Glazed Chicken Kabobs, 90, *91*

    Grilled Garlic-Lime Shrimp Skewers with Vegetables, *120*, 121

    Lamb Kabobs with Tzatziki, 130–31, *131*

Tzatziki, *131*, 131

veal

    Goat Cheese–Stuffed Veal Burgers, *132*, 132–33

    Next-Level Bone-In Veal Chops with Bacon and Bell Pepper Ragu, *134*, 134–35

vegetables

    Grilled Garlic-Lime Shrimp Skewers with Vegetables, *120*, 121

    See also specific vegetables

Velveeta

    Big T's Smoked Mac and Cheese, *158*, 158–60

vinegar, apple cider

    Alabama White BBQ Sauce, 144, *145*

    Basting Liquid, 45

    Classic Sweet BBQ Sauce, *145*, 147

    Mustard-Based BBQ Sauce, 144, *145*

    Vinegar-Based Carolina BBQ Sauce, 146

vinegar, balsamic

    how to make a balsamic reduction, 136

    Next-Level Bone-In Veal Chops with Bacon and Bell Pepper Ragu, *134*, 134–36

vinegar, white

    Al Pastor–Style Pulled Pork, *46*, 46–47

walnuts

    BBQ Banana Split, *188*, 188–89

wings

    Honey-Mustard Glazed Wings, 96, *97*

    Smoked Pickle-Glazed Chicken Wings, *88*, 89

Worcestershire sauce

    Classic Sweet BBQ Sauce, *145*, 147

    Mustard-Based BBQ Sauce, 144, *145*

    Vinegar-Based Carolina BBQ Sauce, 146

yogurt

    Tzatziki, *131*, 131

ABOUT THE AUTHOR

MATT GROARK of Medford Lakes, New Jersey—aka the Meat Teacher—is a physical education and health teacher–turned–culinary instructor who launched his own barbecue business, Groark Boys BBQ, in September 2018. He is married to Kristin and is the father of two boys, Aidric and Nash. The teacher-turned-top-tier-cook quickly made a name for himself, which led to the opportunity to compete on Season 2 of Gordon Ramsay's *Next Level Chef.* Matt boasts over five million followers across his social media platforms. His social media includes all types of cooking and barbecue tips as well as other musings involving his family, daily life, and the occasional sneak peek into his life as a teacher. He is currently focused on his new position in culinary arts and is continuing to grow his barbecue brand.

HarperCollins books may be purchased for educational, business, or sales promotional use. For information, please email the Special Markets Department at SPsales@harpercollins.com.

FIRST EDITION

DESIGNED BY KYLE O'BRIEN

Photography by Kristin Groark

Art credits include:
Highlighter: filmananana © Shutterstock
Chalkboard Pattern: STILLFX © Shutterstock
Illustrations: Abramova Alena © Shutterstock and
Victoria Sergeeva © Shutterstock

Page 10: *Next Level Chef* photos courtesy of
FOX Entertainment © 2023 Fox Media LLC

Library of Congress Cataloging-in-Publication Data has been applied for.

ISBN 978-0-06-328841-6

25 26 27 28 29 LBC 5 4 3 2 1